Touched
by Light

Eyewitness Accounts of Personal Healing

By

Ruth E. Norman
Uriel

UNARIUS ACADEMY OF SCIENCE
El Cajon, California

Touched by Light
Eyewitness Accounts of Personal Healing

Library of Congress Cataloging-in-Publication Data

Norman, Ruth E. - Uriel
   Touched by Light, eyewitness accounts of personal healing, essentials of the healing process.

   Includes bibliography
   ISBN 0935097-37-6

Library of Congress Catalog Card Number 97-60335

   1. Healing   2. Past-life Therapy
   3. Isis and Osiris   4. Reincarnation
        5. Title: Touched by Light

Printed in the United States of America

Ruth E. Norman - URIEL
Cosmic Visionary
Founder, Unarius Academy of Science

Ernest L. Norman - RAPHIEL
Cosmic Visionary
Founder, Unarius Academy of Science

Contents

Foreword

The nature of healing is a dominant theme in the history of mankind. Our literature abounds with expository writings that provide evidence of how individuals have changed their mental and physical dispositions of illness, to be restored and to function with the vigor of good mental and physical health.

The author of this book, Ruth E. Norman, also known as Uriel, is the Co-founder, with Dr. Ernest L. Norman, of the Unarius Academy of Science. The overself or the higher consciousness of Ruth Norman has developed to an advanced Master, and therefore is in-tune with Infinite Intelligence.

Uriel stands for Universal Radiant Infinite Eternal Light. She is the overshadowing consciousness that is making possible the New Age of Spiritual Renaissance, together with countless others who, as Brothers of the Light, are helping to usher our world and planet into the 21st century.

The book, *Touched by Light*, is a remarkable narrative report of persons who have healed themselves by recognizing how they have created their own disease. The results are expressed as a lighter consciousness and a transcendency affecting their ability to feel the love of the Brothers, advanced intelligent minds existing on the higher dimensions of light. The persons whose experiences you will read about speak about their overcoming and healing. Previously they had been reliving the effects of opposing the Light—life as a progressive attainment towards the realization of Cosmic Consciousness.

In their study of the science of life, they now are able to remove the stigma of their disease. They have attested to the wonderful experience of being Touched by the Light, the higher consciousness of spiritual Beings whose motto is "Love in Action."

Over the past forty-three years, the Unarius Academy of Science has been teaching the basic principles of the science of healing. Properly understood, healing is the result of a change in the energies of the cellular structure of the physical anatomy. But most importantly, *healing is the result of a change in the mental climate of the person*—of attitudes based upon old belief systems that had stratified the mind and brain/body system.

In order to truly understand the reality of the healing process, the boundary lines between the past, present and future must be removed to reveal the mental process of consciousness, the database that contains the sum of the past history of the individual. Thus, it is the purpose of each person to learn of themselves in their evolutionary voyage, an infinite vista proclaiming the validity of Spirit.

The Unarius Academy of Science pioneered the teaching of what is now known as "Past Life Therapy." The meaning of this is that the disease of the mind and the brain/body system originated in previous life encounters, in diverse life experiences, lived by any individual. This therapy, a new psychiatry, treats the causative nature of disease, making possible a corrective adjustment to the energy structure of the person. The resultant polarization reverses the degenerative effect of the disease.

The teachings of the healing process, of a corrective and preventive therapy, re-awaken the person to an infinite perspectus of life. Through the process of reincarnation, it is each person's mandate to learn of the creative factors of their mind, to align and connect their higher, creative nature to Infinite Intelligence—the Cosmic Design of life.

If we consider life to be intelligent, and intelligence the sum and total of information based on logic and reason, then healing is no more or no less than the codification of the principles of energy, applicable to each person in their quest for the answers to life's infinite equation.

Antares (Charles Spiegel)
El Cajon, California
February 1, 1997

Preface

You will read in the following pages of paranormal experiences of persons who attended the 13th Interplanetary Conclave of Light, and of references to Uriel, Antares, the Brothers of the Light, and the Hierarchy. These personages are working together in tandem to polarize the consciousness of countless persons who had lost their way on the pathway to Light over a span of many lifetimes.

This pathway is no more or no less than a mandate inscribed within the evolutionary purposes and objectives of all people for the nature of their Spirit Self, their Inner or Higher Self. It is the higher intelligence, supported by an Infinite Creative Intelligence, that provides the libido and drive, life after life and life after death, to find the "pearl of great price."

The following accounts contain experiences of persons enrolled in the past-life therapy classes of the Unarius Academy of Science. Particular focus had been established in the era of Isis and Osiris in Egypt, a history that was relative to each person's past when they lived in Egypt.

There are many legends of Osiris and Isis, who taught about the duality existing in each person, the higher forces of Light and the lower forces of darkness. The dark Forces are represented as persons in positions of authority, as priest-scientists who have continued their arbitrary control over the people of their country.

The prehistory of the civilizations of Yu, Lemuria, Atlantis, and written history up until the present 20th century indicate the battle between the opposite forces of light and darkness.

You will therefore read about Uriel, Antares, and the Brothers who are referred to as having helped particular individuals in their quest for their own spiritual identity—their light force. These personalities are an integral part of the spiritual Brotherhood known as UNARIUS—a universal articulate interdimensional understanding of science.

The quest for the reality of one's spiritual identity has not only been life-long, but lifetime after lifetime. In other words, through the evolutionary processes of reincarnation, the discovery of one's soulic connection has been an ongoing process of education.

The Interplanetary Conclave of Light refers to a two-day symposium presented annually, since 1984, by the Unarius Academy of Science. Its purpose is to re-awaken the people of Earth to the future landing of starships in 2001, as a preparation for the New Age of Spiritual Renaissance.

The physics of reincarnation is exemplified and described in the healing process known as past-life therapy, where one is able to trace the origin of present mental or physical disturbances to discover the reason for one's psychic amnesia.

The deep emotional yet thoughtful realizations and flashbacks of those persons writing their narrative indicate how they have regained their memory associated with the assassination of Isis and Osiris by the priest-scientists of early Egypt. This memory of Isis and Osiris by the priest-scientists of early Egypt is making possible the re-awakening of their spirit nature, through the recognition of their opposition to those who were messengers of the Light. Their psychic liberation is the completion of the healing process.

Uriel represents the Light Forces who work for the betterment of humankind in all disciplines of life. She has appeared and reappeared over thousands of lifetimes as a Wayshower on planet Earth—as a leader, teacher, scientist, poet, and in other expressions of life, reflecting knowledge of the higher orders of the mind.

Touched by Light, Eyewitness Accounts of Personal Healing is important, not only because it validates the psychodynamics of reincarnation, but it also verifies the principles of the science of healing. Humankind, individually and as a whole, is reliving the past, a karmic indenture, so to speak, wherein every person is reflecting the sum and total of his or her own personal past. Therefore, we consider the articles of the individuals included to be of a landmark and pioneering nature. They have seen the reality of Light, the encompassing, overshadowing, inter-penetrating force of Cosmic Intelligence.

Kevin Kennedy

"Liar!" the voice yelled in my consciousness. "Liar," it rang out again. What was this voice? And why was it so strong in my mind?

For the past two weeks I've been attempting to write up my experiences of our wonderful Interplanetary Conclave of Light; and yet, each time I sat down, I felt blocked off—no inflow—feeling as if I would just be making something up to write about it. At first I rationalized, saying to myself, "I'm a terrible writer anyway, others will do a much better job."

And yet, as I listened to each student relate from their heart the tremendous benefit from the Conclave, I kept feeling guilty and negative. I couldn't put my finger on the reason why I couldn't write about my experiences.

Then, last Thursday night as I studied, the recognition came full force of why I was having so much resistance, "Liar!"

I had spent years in the Isis and Osiris lifetime telling such untruths that I was faced with the monster of my own making. I was having to change the momentum of those energies put forth in a negative, negative way. I had been a spokesperson for the negative forces, and now I was on the receiving end of these energies! I felt a spider's web had ensnared me, then was ripped away as this realization sank into my consciousness.

Suddenly, it was as if a cloud had been lifted in my mind and I knew I could share what this weekend meant to me.

It was love and effort coming to full bloom. I had the tremendous opportunity to help Antares with the brochure for the Interplanetary Conclave of Light, with the banners and signs, and help in giving a multimedia presentation on Saturday. I lived for six months with this celebration, yet nothing seemed to prepare me for the onrush of power projected by the Brothers on Sunday, October 13, during the flag procession of the 33 worlds of the Interplanetary Confederation. I was the emcee for the flag procession, welcoming our visitors to the landing site and greeting the polarities of the 33 worlds.

As I welcomed our guests, I suddenly was overcome by the realization and awareness that we were not alone in our celebration. I felt and saw in my mind's eye the Brothers and Sisters of these other worlds enjoined with us, projecting their love and consciousness to Earth to help in the change and up-going of our planet.

The feeling is beyond words. I felt at one with all things and saw the golden thread of life flowing between these students, that love that ties the universe together. I have never felt so proud of my fellow students and what was being accomplished on that day, for I saw our present and our future—a future of joined consciousness in Spirit!

It seemed to be over in a flash—the beautiful banner procession, the release of the 33 snow-white doves as harbingers of our Love and Light to the Brothers of the Confederation, and the peace of mind coming forth for taking part in a positive way in the change of planet Earth—a sight and joy never to be forgotten.

I must say what a privilege it was to work with our Brother, Antares. The closeness of oscillation and positive involvement gave me balance and a clarity of consciousness I have never experienced before. Now more than ever, I know this is just the beginning. As Uriel stated, "The future of the earth world is positive, progressive, I promise you!" And now I know I'm a part of that future.

Crystal Hampton

Weeks prior to the 13th Annual Interplanetary Conclave of Light, I was working out a past lifetime; the Isis and Osiris cycle designates the time and place. This cycle was a historical tragedy of which the world's history books contain no thorough recollection. Unarius has retrieved the histories of Light Beings who have journeyed to this planet to enlighten the atrophying minds of human beings and has restored the truth from past ages, searched for by almost all people. The existence of the Light Beings, who live purposefully within a civilization to teach, heal, and breathe into the plasma field of life itself infinitely creative mental energies, was not meant to be a secret. Instead, this fact of life was distorted, changed, and in most cases extinguished from earth's history by the negative Forces. Two such Beings graced our planet in the now 20th century. Isis and Osiris returned as Ruth and Ernest Norman.

Lack of usage of the mind to evolve into higher dimensions of concept and understanding causes a person to shrivel up and die spiritually. If we shut the door of our mind with limited concepts, no new intelligence develops. At this moment in time I am filled to overflowing with what Unarius is!! I am so overwhelmed to know there is the doorway to a future so highly intelligent, filled with unfathomable love. This doorway is any one of the Unarius books, as they are a living, breathing consciousness that revives and rebirths the mind that listens and conceives meaning. Unarius is an open doorway that leads to a vast, inner universe whose invisible presence makes life present on any earth world or galaxy.

The 13th Annual Interplanetary Conclave of Light was a peak cycle, as great energies from these inner dimensions could actually be felt. For some, it was a time of rich and immediate transformation, as his or her preparation for this time made them more open. For others, the Conclave was but an introduction to life; definitive energies received and seeded for future evolutions. It is the power that makes a Unarius event unlike any other, and this power has the ability to change the direction of one's evolution. This was my experience as I sat within this healing mechanism, the Interplanetary Conclave. Very much like being within a starship from another world, the two-day event encompassed totally my physical body and touched every part of my mind.

The great tug of war that existed between an old world and a new world was what overtook me in the past, as I had set out to be a devoted student to the teachings of Isis and Osiris. The murder of these two Light Beings stopped and waylaid this future craft of consciousness from landing, bringing with it a new and positive life. I had been a student of Isis, but I allowed the pressure from the negative forces to enter my mind and take me over, the negative forces, whose plot it was to wipe her from the face of the earth, along with Osiris and their spiritual teachings. In listening to a rumor and not making a stand against it, the destructive forces can enter and do their work, making of you an instrument in their intent. This was my experience, listening and not doing anything to oppose the force taking hold; insidious as it was in my thoughts, I found myself caught up in the most nightmarish past a person could possibly imagine or, to me, endure.

It has not been simple to come to a full recognition and acceptance of my deeds in that lifetime when I turned on those two great illumined Teachers. The shock and imprint of that eventful day, when they were murdered by a drugged, "zombied" clan of followers, has lingered in my memory in ways that only amnesia would provide some solace. And amnesia it has been, of how I too joined forces with that mob as these two were sliced, diced and bludgeoned to death. Even that day of the procession of the Interplanetary Flags, the highlight of our two-day event, I had a flashback. As we turned the corner and saw an assemblage of people sitting in the desert-like terrain, I felt I stepped back in time for a moment. I felt haunted with the sight. I was sickened with what I remembered, the alignment of the crowd implementing the plot to kill. I remembered the cup that had been passed to drink from, a drug made from herbs that would "zombify" the would-be killers, making it easy for them to carry out the plot. The setting for the second day of the Conclave, the landing site, where the terrain is the dry natural earth or desert-like terrain, served for a perfect attunement to this past.

The greatest thing of all is the opportunity for healing. The cup now offered is one of pure understanding—a long deep look back into this past once more to gain the realization of the error I committed in this travesty. I was against Spirit.

The resistance was great up until the last week or so of the preparation of the Conclave. The words of Antares rang clear as he spoke at one of our class sessions, to me in the back row who listened on, and had not truly been involved with all the planning for this annual event. He said I could be a part of the group if I wanted to be, and not to give up, on myself essentially. I had no thoughts of ever giving up on myself or my striving to understand and gain Spirit. His words were a jolt, and public deflation can be wonderful therapy if done with pure intent and intelligence—the purpose and motivation from which his direct comment was made to me. It worked. I knew I had been separating myself and even had resistance to attending each class three times a week, which I'd done for many years.

During the two days of the 13th Annual Interplanetary Conclave of Light, I was less concerned with myself. I focused upon the information given, and thereby I felt the pulse of my true self and the inner dimensions. I felt the Interplanetary Conclave of Light a real, viable force, and I felt myself rise above my material concerns to enjoy and journey. I was able to look into my problems and had many pivotal realizations. I had allowed myself to slip backwards. I'd been giving myself over to the earth day material life. For some months previous to the Conclave my concern with work and home life was becoming an all-consuming life of itself. I had not taken time to turn my thoughts away from it all to study, the simplest, most concrete means by which I could rise above my obsessions.

The many changes I went through in the days leading up to and during this event strengthened my true desires and objectives with my inner self and true purpose. I am forever grateful for this opportunity to express my feelings, the difference between being separated from the Light and being joined with it, how these special events are set up for us to make a new and higher conjunction of consciousness as the projected energies are received. I've learned that I must be open in order to receive this consciousness that Unarius opens the cosmic curtain to, and I am eager to learn and to help in the many projects provided for all students, projects that serve to tune attention away from the material life and add energies to the psychic anatomy that build integration with the inner planes and the minds of the Light Beings.

Over all, during the Conclave I felt I was in an advanced class on the inner planes, my past, present, and future were revealed. It was not a time of sitting back and enjoying festivities. I felt a contrast within myself, and what I felt were the soothing waters of spirit within a tired, physical frame. I had not been giving enough attention to the ultimate purpose for which I am here. This event and celebration is a most ingenious means for which progress is engineered, right then in the now, moving me forward due to the many realizations I opened myself up to receive, pushing the false ego aside.

I recall one day, just shortly after Antares had spoken to me in class, that I sat at my desk at work. I had been put on hold by a person I had spoken to on the phone. A song was heard over the phone. I recognized the melody and the song itself. I listened to the words, and they said, "You've got a friend in me . . . .You've got a friend in me . . . . You've got a friend in me." Suddenly, something most wondrous occurred. I slipped out of my normal work state of mind and rode a carrier wave of the purest, loving, tranquil and beautiful energy right into the thoughts of Antares. I knew this was his new frequency that I'd contacted. An inner knowing flooded me, how this was his love that I had contacted in his expression as the Teacher. It was one of those proofs that no one can dissuade you from; it was just as real as knowing what the sun feels like or what a rose looks like and smells like when its fragrance is sensed. It was the love of the Brothers, the Light Beings; this level of dimension that is always there surrounding and interlacing my life. Just to tune into it, it happened so effortlessly, just like slipping into a tepid pool of clear water, imbued with infinite love and absolute freedom from a physical body. For this is my lesson, the lesson of physical and spiritual worlds, the past and the future? I choose . . . the Future . . . !

Lani Calvert

As the march progressed in the hot sun, I checked the rank and file. The usual problems were apparent: the lazy, the clowns, those who resented and challenged my authority. I would have to ride them. Yes, the scene was familiar. It happened in many countries, on many planets, with a variety of costumes and levels of weapon sophistication, but the energy remained the same. The same problems cropped up, despite disciplinary measures devised to physically or psychologically control the troops. In spite of this, frequency relationship and military victories were sufficient that I continually found myself in similar positions with similar problems life after life.

As if coming up with a battle plan and handling troop morale wasn't enough, I was given extra duties, or I took them on in order to maintain my status and cull the favor of whoever happened to be giving me orders. However, I was used to taking and giving orders, so in spite of the stress, all seemed "normal."

So much for flashbacks. In the present, besides the routine time and consciousness demands of my regular job, facilitating Unarius classes, handling seven (and pursuing more) Public Access stations, the choral workbook class, the yearly demands of the Conclave of Light parade, and this year the physically exhausting work preparing raw land for the second day of Conclave events, the latest addition to my plate was a planning meeting for Conclave speakers. As a student, I knew the opportunity was another chance to turn around my past, but at the moment it just seemed like more work, more responsibility. Yeah, I had a bad attitude.

Thus, after a hard day "attacking" dense brush at the

land, I went to the first meeting because it was expected. As potential speakers, we were queried on possible topics. While I didn't feel particularly inspired, I voiced what ideas came to me. Coming from my conscious mind, they were equivalent to my strategies or battle plans of the past. Everything I said was "wrong." It was emphasized that one should speak on a topic one had experience with and not just give a "book report" of things one had read. However, I didn't have any first-hand or physical experience with UFOs, space travel, the Muons or the planets of the Interplanetary Confederation . . . I felt confused and at a loss.

The ideas I voiced provided a conduit for mild shocks, as the Director wasted no words in declaring the state of my consciousness. In front of my peers, I was asked not to be a speaker. In a past life, this represented being demoted or it was publicly stated why I was unqualified to handle an important speech or campaign. In the present, part of me was quick to rationalize in order to lessen the ego deflation; no great loss, I had too much to do and it was one less thing I had to think about and prepare for. The other part of me tried to analyze what was going on and to stay as objective as possible. This small opening of objectivity allowed more of the past to come into play, so I could look deeper.

By the end of the meeting, the Director suggested I could talk about "Orion." I was immediately struck by a certain dark humor in the suggestion, as the grim associations conjured up by the word so aptly outpictured my current state of mind. While "Orion" is a general and vast subject covering millions of years, the images which came to mind were of a military commander and battle scenes. Yes, that was a topic I could speak about from experience. Countless relivings and realizations gave me a definite psychic reservoir to draw from. So many lifetimes in similar positions had molded my perspective of life to where I approached it as a battle to be won. I consciously or unconsciously strategized how to conquer the opposing forces and motivate the troops.

Over the ensuing week, I felt a pressure to come up with my "battle plan," a specific topic which would both satisfy the Director and hold audience interest. I debated how I could orient the subject so that it was not too heavy.

Due to the previous deflation, at the next meeting I had more trepidation about speaking my mind. Ultimately, I forged ahead, deciding it was better to know if I was on track or not. In presenting my topic, I supported it with the statement that it was a subject people were currently interested in. My receptivity to whatever I needed to know again provided the conduit for a jolt of energy in the form of the response. "That's not the way we do things! You don't lower your consciousness to the level of the audience; you speak from spirit!" I was once again asked not to speak. This was salt in the wound, and I recoiled. While in afterthought it was stated that the parade was enough for me to deal with (and it was), by this time I saw it as a conciliatory statement to keep me from going too far down with the deflation.

I knew the Director was right. I was reliving the past. I had used my conscious mind to try to come up with a topic instead of being open to "spirit" and channeling the Intelligence of Higher Beings. Depression set in. My higher and lower selves began a personal battle of Armageddon within me. The first attack focused on the weakest flanks—my insecurities. Why was I allowed to facilitate classes if I wasn't considered capable of doing a lecture? After 12 years of study, I had failed in my objective. Why did I remain here as a student if I couldn't even learn the basics?

My counter attack was to keep doing the best I could. I kept plugging away: writing, asking questions, being as supportive as possible of whatever projects I was involved with, and analyzing.

The first small victory, in this ongoing battle with my lower self, came shortly after the second meeting. It came from the knowledge of what old thought patterns were in operation. From all my flashbacks of military positions in past lives, I realized that I was either accustomed or programmed to receive and follow orders from superiors in command. There is a definite element of security that comes from being told what to do. I was comfortable with orders; give me a physical task to accomplish and I'll charge right in! However, this also generates dependency and weakens one's ability to think for oneself. Suddenly I was faced with the necessity of developing, strengthening and utilizing connections with higher Beings and my own higher self in order to proceed.

I began to see glimpses of previous lifetimes where Master Teachers had pointed out this same weakness that I needed to overcome in order to go forward in my evolution. Rather than accept their wisdom, I had criticized these spiritual teachers for daring to tell me my modus operandi was flawed. Some lives I simply withdrew from their presence. More often, I helped to get rid of them in order to silence the voices that threatened my self-image, shattered my ego, or removed the false platforms I'd built to try to rise above my insecurities. I thus saw where I had lost this same battle of Armageddon many times and that was why it felt so intense.

These realizations helped me to identify the real enemy and take advantage of subsequent opportunities to rectify the mistakes of the past. I started to analyze my experiences and emotions in the context of the past I was in-phase with. While doing physical labor with others to transform sandstone and dead brush into a beautiful setting for the celebration, I was able to view the contrasting effects of following orders versus following one's inner voice. In the human mirrors around me, I saw the debilitating and deleterious effects of people giving and receiving orders, of people pushing or trying to control others in the tasks at hand. On the other hand, when all participants were allowed or encouraged to follow their inspiration and take responsibility for their own reactions, so much more was accomplished! The future of earth was revealed as everyone worked in harmony, in a unified consciousness, with no one having to give orders.

I accepted that my former modus operandi was causing me to keep fighting the same battles over and over and I was determined to change. This allowed me to open up my channel to receive direction from higher sources. Sunday, October 13th, the day of the parade, provided a variety of experiences of the effects of this inner connection.

Despite ongoing preparations and various realizations, it wasn't until Sunday morning that I noticed other students were taking charge of certain details of the parade. I consciously felt relieved and realized I'd mentally taken on a weight of responsibility for making sure everything was done. My first thought was that I should have delegated more. Yet, reflecting back, I realized that when I was open to help, it was there without my having to request or monitor it.

In the afternoon, buses filled with conclave attendees headed for the landing site. People carrying flags in the parade were all on the second bus. The TV camera crew covering the event had decided to ride in this bus as well in order to conduct interviews en route. The interviewer logically assumed all carriers were students or "veterans" of previous parades. This was not the case. As "luck" would have it, the flag carrier interviewed was the one who had had the least contact with Unarius.

When asked how he felt about UFOs and the premise of the day's events, his response included the words "strange," "weird," etc. A long-term student and I looked despairingly across the bus at each other as we listened. I mentally cringed in anticipation of the sound-bites I foresaw the media choosing to use, out of a whole day of filming positive events. The other student stated vehemently several times to me, loudly enough for the interviewer to hear, "Tell her you want to do an interview!" I felt uncomfortable butting in, knowing the media would perceive that we were trying to draw them away, as if to cover information we didn't want revealed. Such information would be all the more enticing to them.

Instead, I knew I had to change my consciousness. My concerns were adding to the problem I perceived. I mentally viewed the man as a spark of the Infinite and saw his flame being kindled by Infinite Intelligence. I turned to face him and had a genuine smile of encouragement and support. His statements changed in frequency. He polarized negatives with positives, stating, for example, that despite how others might view things, he was excited and supportive of all that was going on. It struck me that my efforts to "see" his true inner self resonated with a universal, higher frequency energy and then became a strengthening factor between us rather that a debilitating one.

When we reached the landing site, the flag carriers got off the bus and gathered at the top of the hill to begin the procession. In spite of all efforts and planning to keep everything happening in a tight sequence of events, there was cause for concern. The small, model spaceship that traditionally houses the doves used in the celebration, was "on stage" from the beginning. In order to keep the doves cool in the typical October heat waves, they were supposed to be loaded right before the audience arrived. The audience was now seated and I learned that not only had the doves not been loaded but they had not even arrived. The cordless phone/beeper system we'd arranged to maintain contact was not working and three of the flag carriers were still down the hill at the stage area with no way to page them. The camera crews were standing by and prior experience told me the flag carriers could easily become restless, tired or otherwise out of tune as we waited in the hot sun.

At this point, I had my next experience with the interdimensional, directive energy source. Another student served as a wonderful polarity in suggesting that I lead everyone in an "attunement." While I had wanted to do this, I had not thought there would be enough time and it had been forgotten in my concerns of the moment. I gratefully gathered everyone.

In "attuning," I lost consciousness of the mounting material concerns. In shifting my thoughts to our brothers and sisters on other physical and non-physical planets, I mentally adjusted my receiver to pick up higher frequency thought waves. In this timeless, spaceless dimension, the reception was clear and instantaneous. I voiced the images that were impressed in my consciousness, in order to help anyone who might have trouble with their own reception and to unify us. I suggested that they each contact the polarity whom they represented today so they could serve as a good interplanetary conduit during the parade. I was aware of the many higher Beings in attendance and especially Uriel, the overshadowing Intelligence of the former physical Director of Unarius. This celebration had been initiated with her beneficent contact with all of the 32 worlds of the Interplanetary Confederation. I saw how absolutely necessary it was to nurture the inner connection with all my spiritual teachers, guides, Brothers and Sisters. Earth is a school and what I was learning and experiencing this day is what life is all about! By the time we finished, the three missing flag carriers approached. The doves had been loaded and we were able to give a trumpet blast to signal the start of the procession.

The next experience came at the very end of the parade,

when all the flag carriers were lined up along the edge of the road, near the tent. Their instructions during rehearsals had been to remain in place until the last of the audience had passed by and then we would be the last ones to file into the tent. It took a good while for this to happen. I could see people starting to fidget and break in consciousness. However, the Director had not yet come by and I wanted him to see this last part of the parade. The thought came to me to run down the line or shout to people to "hold the ranks!" until he had passed by. I smiled and shooed the thought along, as it was easy to see where it was coming from. Ultimately, I kept my thoughts on the importance of why they needed to stay put and that our mutual development involved learning to communicate mentally and be in tune with the greater plan. I was pleased when everyone was in tune enough to remain the extended time.

Under an archway of trumpeteers, the flag carriers followed everyone into a large, white tent for the last of the day's events. Our Director made the mental interface with the advanced Beings in the higher dimensions and a clear broadcast was voiced. Near the end, the distinct frequency Intelligence of Uriel came through. Since Uriel continues (in the non-atomic dimensions) as the true Director of the Unarius Academy, this type of interjection of a direct communication has occurred with many transmissions in the past. However, I honestly did not always feel the change in frequency. This time, I truly felt a difference when it happened. It resonated through my body. Uncontrollable sobs followed. I had the thought and overwhelming feeling that I finally did something right!

Looking back, I can see that the strong emotions were due to the fact that I had just won a major battle with my lower self. After all these lifetimes, I had stopped fighting this particular battle with my teachers and my higher self.

I was able to take firm steps in constructing a new future instead of continuing to relive the virtual reality of former lives. I made the right choice; I turned the right direction; I went forward instead of turning my back; I opened up to spirit for inspiration and guidance . . . Uriel was smiling!

Now when I flash back to the parade, I can appreciate my ability to see with new eyes, without the emotionally crippling residue of past life experiences superimposed over the present. I can finally rewrite the chapter dealing with the battle that re-occurred in my biography life after life.

As I stepped forward to begin the procession, I felt the warmth of a spiritual sun warming my being and psychically lighting the way. I did not need to look behind me; I sensed the unified consciousness of my brothers and sisters and knew their steps were guided by a "still, small voice." The former disciplinary problems were no longer reflected back to me. Because I was viewing the best in each person, I did not find any clowns or laziness. No one challenged my authority because I did not project any. It was a timeless experience. While we were literally walking on the highlands of the former civilization of Lemuria, the parade was a culmination of countless marches into battle in the past and a preview of countless processionals of the future on atomic and non-atomic planets. Our uniforms had been replaced with airy, non-restrictive garments which reflected each individual's creative nature. My weapon had been replaced by a trumpet to herald the beginning of a new age. The only disciplinary measures that had to be applied were to myself; to take responsibility for my own reactions and problems. Because of this small victory in my personal battle of Armageddon, I look forward to similar positions of opportunity and new problems to overcome in future lives, as each provides a stepping stone to self-mastery and a more creative, fulfilling way of life.

As for waiting for a person of superior rank to tell me how to proceed, my mental reception has been upgraded to receive inspiration from a higher frequency source. In facilitating Unarius classes, I've lost many former concerns I had about "my" classes. As I seem to have less and less time to "prepare," I've been forced to rely more completely on the advanced Beings who are the true teachers of the Unarius classes. Since I don't know any more (and probably less) than my fellow human beings, the capability to lead, help or inspire depends on my receptivity to an advanced Brotherhood of Beings whose wisdom far surpasses any in this atomic dimension. Thus, while such is quite the opposite from the traditional teaching methods taught today, the more I get my conscious mind out of the way and "tune-up" my reception, the better the classes.

The 13th Annual Conclave of Light was, for me, an opportunity to identify and step out of the darkness of the ignorance of my past and to experience the lighted contrast of my future. It is still a constant battle for me to stay alert and to break old, habitual ways of doing things. Yet, once I am resolved to take a firm step to change, the actual process of attunement is effortless. It is uplifting and rewarding in countless, unforeseen ways. All is already known and already done. When I am receptive to Infinite Creative Intelligence, the Master Plan—"God," if you will, then I become a co-creator of a positive future, rather than an enforcer of my negative past.

May McFalls

As I walked down the hill with the flag representing the planet Dal in my hands, tears of joy and sadness ran down my cheeks—tears of joy, because I could feel the love of Uriel and the Brothers welling up and overflowing within me. The emotions of anger I had been experiencing, particularly during the last two days, melted away; they seemed so terribly petty. I now experienced joy; I know no other way to describe my emotion for being here in El Cajon and participating, as best I can, in the preparation for the landing of spaceships on planet Earth. At that moment there was no doubt whatsoever in my mind that there would be a landing in 2001!

How proud and honored I was to be carrying that flag. The transcendency increased as we continued to walk toward the audience and the spaceship. Each segment of the program seemed as a step up—the music, the trumpeteers, the reading of the Proclamation, the welcome extended to the representative of each planet, and the release of the 33 white doves—the finale. What beauty to see the doves fly about, what inner beauty to realize what they represented. As I stood there, I wondered if the Brothers were approving of the physical display of our appreciation. I floated down the road to take my place in forming a receiving line for our guests. This whole part of the celebration seemed to pass by in just a few seconds.

Again, I was filled with love as Antares received the message from Uriel and the Brothers that evening. Their words of love and encouragement filled the tent and lifted me. As is usual for me, in that state of consciousness, I had only conceived a few sentences of the transmission and already was looking forward to the printed form. The tears flowed again as Uriel, through Antares, gave roses to several deserving students.

On Saturday, when the evening talks began, I was trying to get over the anger I felt because my car had been towed away. The anger had subsided, somewhat, when Barbara Jane started her talk. I noted that her mannerisms were different than usual, and I listened more closely to what she was saying. She was telling us about her dream in which Uriel had given her a rose. As she said, "Uriel asked me to give this rose to each one of you." she extended her arm to do so, and I felt my whole body vibrate, particularly in the solar plexus. It took me by great surprise! I questioned, how could I be in the pits of these negative emotions, one minute, and then be able to feel Uriel's Love in that manner, the next? I have had the same type experience a few other times, but never when I felt I was in such a negative state of mind.

As Gary took the microphone and uttered his first sentences, I could feel his nervousness. Mentally, I gave him my support. Gradually, I felt he was more at ease and had more confidence in himself. As I listened to Marian give her talk, I could see and appreciate her growth during the two years that I have been here. She seemed so shy two years ago.

These events were in no way the limit of my experiences associated with this Conclave weekend.

Later, as I was reading the printed copy of the transmission, I highlighted several sentences that stood out for me, they were:

1. "When you have conceived of the reality of the higher Self, you will then experience your at-one-ment with your inner self."

2. "One who has not learned of his own nature thinks that someone else has the truth."

3. "This means that you contain all of these factors within yourself, but you have looked in the wrong direction

for answers to your life. The answers can only be found by looking within."

In the classes that followed, several students read their paper describing their experience of the Conclave of Light; Jack's hit home with me. As I had not finished my paper, I felt I wanted to mention how his sharing affected me; however it did not all gel at one time, and my paper changed several times.

Jack told of having a problem and asking the Brothers for help. He received that help! He had, like other students, conceived the three principles mentioned above. I have not, and that, in a nut shell, was the reason for my intermingled tears of sadness as I walked down the hill. There was guilt: guilt that I have not accomplished all that I am capable of, guilt that I should be a better student, guilt that I could be helping more, guilt that . . . ; I could go on, but the three principles extracted from the transmission tell it all—I have looked outside myself for answers, looked outside myself for truth, my truth. Only I have the answers to my guilt and frustrations, and only I can clean out the debris and allow the Light to shine through.

Most of my realizations during the Isis and Osiris cycle were not of that cycle, but were of what I feel to be harmonics of that cycle, for I was in-tune with the atrocities of World War II and the concentration camps. At the very first planning meeting for the Conclave, I reacted to all of us being transported to the landing site in buses, being dropped off and then picked up after the celebration. It was not until we had been dropped off, on the day of the celebration, that it dropped into my consciousness that the buses represented the trains taking prisoners to the work camps, which in reality were the gas chambers. Several other pieces then fell into place.

As I write this, another piece falls into place. In preparing for the celebration, I helped bury the electric lines at the landing site. This was the reliving of me helping to to bury the gas lines to the gas chamber during that past.

At the celebration, the tent represented a gas chamber to me. It was out in the middle of nowhere. We were all gathered inside in this small area, with the great outdoors just outside the door. We were prisoners; we could not leave until the buses were ready to take us back home.

While we were planting the oleanders, I helped with several tasks, but I ended up packing the dirt around each plant and "beautifying" the surrounding land by spreading out the dirt. I became aware I was burying something and was trying to conceal the fact that something was buried there.

At the landing, site during the celebration, I reacted strongly to the decorations placed around the "Welcome Space Brothers in 2001" spaceship sign on the hill. The ground beneath was decorated with a blanket of green artificial turf, with bunches of flowers placed around it. It was a perfect grave; I could not even look at it. This was the one thing that symbolized the Isis and Osiris cycle to me. The grave represented their demise, and the spaceship, situated appropriately above the grave, represented that spaceship 10,000 years ago. As it has been related to us, the Space Brothers watched from their spaceship as Isis and Osiris were killed. The fact that I could not even look at it tells me I was there with Isis and Osiris in a negative way. Intellectually, I can see the harmonics of both events, mankind's continual fight for superiority and mankind's continual effort to do away with anything and everything he does not understand. However I cannot, at the present time, conceive it all.

Not in the two years I have been here, has there been a time that my emotions have flip flopped from on extreme to the other or that I seemed unable to control them.

Carol Robinson

As plans for this year's Interplanetary Conclave of Light began to take shape during meetings at the Lighthouse, I found myself feeling engulfed in a tornado of negative energy. There was something different about this year's celebration, a feeling that I had not experienced before. I reacted to several things: the increase in the cost for attending the Conclave, the projected increase in the number of attendees, and the setting chosen for the celebration, a barren hillside which offered no facilities for even basic amenities. I realized that tremendous effort and great expense would be required to convert this chaparral into a suitable setting for the yearly celebration. Yet each excuse that I could name did not really account for my continuing negative feelings and resistance to preparing for the annual Conclave, for each of these excuses could be resolved.

As the days passed, the brochure to announce this event to the world was finished and mailed to almost 100,000 potential attendees. Surely it would attract a large number of people interested in preparing for the landing of spaceships on Earth. Advertisements were placed in strategic magazines and newspapers. The word was now out.

I felt as though the dye was cast; there would be no turning back now. We would celebrate the 13th Interplanetary Conclave as outlined in the brochure, but beneath the surface of my mind resistance continued. I really didn't want a public gathering to witness this event, the re-enactment of a past tragedy wherein I had openly lead a mob in a brutal attack upon both Osiris and Isis and their remaining followers.

The focus of the preparations then shifted to the land

purchased by Uriel as the future landing site in Jamul, California. Water and power would be needed, grading would be required for the tent, dining, and areas for parking. And then there would be the need for clean-up, clearing, planting, and beautifying the barren hillside below the spaceship, all would be essential.

Frank and I drove out to the landing site. I was in-tune with Egypt at the time that Isis and Osiris were the rulers of the upper and lower kingdoms. As I walked the land, I felt an excitement somewhat similar to that which a settler might feel as he was deciding the layout of his land for future development, but I was really out-picturing my desire for power over Egypt, for a position of power and the adulation of the Egyptian people.

When Osiris and Isis announced their plans to depart on the spacecraft which would soon be arriving, bringing Brothers from another planet to Egypt who would, in their place, become the leaders of Egypt, I felt betrayed. I had looked forward to the day when I would naturally inherit a position among the future leaders of Egypt. I was living with Isis as one of the family, and had worked diligently for this position, which I feel I had earned. But, as I lived with the Gods, I began to feel that I was as the Gods, of their mental development, and from this belief assumed a posture that was untrue. I felt superior to others, jealous of Isis, and was privately suppressing an inner knowing that I was not what I was openly pretending to be.

In the present, as in Egypt over 10,000 years ago, Isis became aware of my ulterior motives and obsession for power and she exposed my masquerading as well as my negative influence on Seth. She told me to immediately leave the household. I was to take with me my immediate needs and plan to return only to pick up my remaining belongings. I left, but my determination to get even grew without bounds. So, when Seth proposed his plan to gain control of Egypt by eliminating Osiris and Isis, I saw the opportunity to take my revenge. I was in total agreement with his plan.

In the days and months that followed my departure from the Lighthouse, I plotted my return to power; only in failure did I begin to acknowledge the reality of my great resentment towards Isis. I wanted the inner qualities she had developed, the grace, the kindness, the inner awareness to understand those around her. I wanted to be as she, but always felt inadequate. And I was inadequate, if to be adequate meant being able to fill the shoes of Isis.

Eventually, I was also able to see that I valued above all else the status that I gained by my association with these Gods of Egypt. As I watched my thoughts they told a story of my selfish concern for power, for control, and for the material aspects of life. What I wanted, and saw in the being of Isis, I had not yet developed; so my feelings of inadequacy grew to such an extent that I began to believed myself to be something more than I was. I had not taken advantage of the opportunity to learn, to build within my inner self the mental constructs that would eventually open to me the inner vision and wisdom that was Isis.

As I accepted this more realistic position, the symptoms of a cold and an ear infection began to diminish. I became more willing to become a part of the present efforts to prepare for the landing of the Brothers; in fact, I began to enjoy being a part of the preparations.

Yes, the preparation of the landing site did require great effort, but it was an effort that made it possible to see the reality of the past and gain, with each trip to the land, a greater clarity of consciousness. The dried and decaying limbs of trees and bush that were removed and disposed of, and the caked-on dirt along the roadside brought to mind the bloody remains of the carnage that had occurred in this past era. Even the polluted water supply and the new electrical connection had symbolic meaning that helped to reawaken additional memories, additional negations.

On the last Saturday that I spent at the land, I felt a need to have a hose with which to wash down the road, but this feeling too faded as I recognized that my need was, in reality, to remove the remaining guilt reflected by this remaining evidence of the past.

The developing plot against the lives of Osiris and Isis paved the way for Seth to assume the leadership of Egypt, but even my support for Seth lasted only as long as his position would serve my needs. An assassin arrived from the east to execute a subplot engineered by Horus, who had been away from Egypt at this time. I knew where the assassin would be staying. Early the next morning, and while all were asleep, I opened the door of the palace to admit the assassin who then carried out his task, the murder of Seth. (In the present my need was to deliver copies of the book *Monographs of Galactic Intelligence*.)

These plots and subplots grew unbridled by logic and reason because of attitudes devoid of Spirit. Such atrocities are difficult to accept, but it is equally difficult to accept that with the murder of Osiris and Isis and the departure of the Brothers Earth was plunged into darkness, for the Light to illuminate the spirit of humanity and the intelligence which would have been guidance for the continued leadership of Egypt and the world was, for a long time, dimmed.

As the weekend of the 13th Interplanetary Conclave of Light grew closer, I could feel a new sense of unity within the Unarius nucleus. There was a feeling of camaraderie, a sense of togetherness. Classes, which were always our opportunity to share our insights and realizations, reflected this new openness.

As I stood upon the hillside waiting for the signal to begin the procession, there was a stillness. Looking out beyond the western horizon was to look into infinity. The love of Osiris and Isis and of the whole Unarius Brotherhood seemed to be raining all around, and in this moment, when time seemed to be suspended, I felt at-one with this Infinite Love. The Light of truth, which I had previously wished to eliminate and from which I had tried to hide, had, in this moment of attunement, engulfed my being. I shall not ever be the same.

Soon all was in readiness. Leading the parade was the Space-Cad surrounded by the trumpeteers. Those who carried a flag representing one of the planets of the Confederation followed. There was no curtain to be raised, yet as I walked I felt as though I was passing through what had been a barrier, and was now about to enter upon a new stage, a new life.

How different this years celebration was from those of other years. The change that I experienced within myself was revitalizing and Uriel's words to us during the transmission meant so much to me; they were reassuring. They were, as always, the Fountainhead of Love. This Conclave had become a successful turnabout of this negative past, and I could feel the joy of the Infinite for our successful overcoming. And certainly I never expected to receive a rose from Uriel, for I had done less in a physical way to participate in this years celebration than in other years. Actually, I felt that I had not really made a contribution.

But it was Antares' vision, his willingness to follow his inner promptings, that became the example of the workings of Spirit and the manner of its manifesting for the benefit of we who have followed his example in the past. My overcoming could not have come about without his greater overcoming preceding my own. He has been the trailblazer, so to speak, so that during the past several months he could be the visionary and act as a guide to lead us through the underbrush, through the predictable contortions of mind as we encountered the artifacts of this past and our resistance to their emotional impact.

Barbara Jane Rogers

The Interplanetary Conclave of Light was a wonderful, transcending, educational experience, which truly reflected the tremendous outpouring of love and Infinite intelligence of the Unarius Brotherhood, as well as a new group consciousness among those who participated. Each of the presentations and musical expressions seemed to build up to the magnificent Parade of Flags of the 33 Confederation planets and the release of the 33 white doves held, for the first time, at the future landing site for the 33 Confederation starships. Yet the most meaningful of all was the transmission from Uriel, which strengthened our commitment as members of a brotherhood of man to function as an integrated whole toward the spiritual awakening of the earth people.

While taking part in the preparation for the Conclave, and reading *Preparation for the Landing*, I began to appreciate in a deeper way the importance and magnitude of this Unarius mission to prepare earth people for the arrival of spacecraft from the 32 planets of the Interplanetary Confederation and for the great spiritual awakening beginning to unfold on Earth. I felt so appreciative to be a part of this mission, contributing in whatever way I can, and to be a student under the tutelage of such Masters as Uriel, Raphiel, Michiel, etc.

For me, the Conclave of Light really began early Saturday morning with a tremendous psychic experience which demonstrated to me the tremendous love and overshadowing guidance of the Unarius Brotherhood, especially of Uriel. As I went to sleep Friday night, my thoughts were focused on the presentation I was to make on the topic "The 21st Century and the Age of Spiritual

Renaissance." I knew I needed to overcome certain fears in order to be a channel for the Brothers. Before awakening, while in hypcognic state, I suddenly found myself enveloped in a cocoon of warm, scintillating white light, feeling an inner sense of oneness and heightened awareness of my true spiritual purpose. I then felt this overwhelming love fill my consciousness, and as I opened my eyes, I saw Uriel standing before me in a shimmering gold and silver gown. In her hand was a beautiful red rose. As she reached out to give me the rose, she said "Take this rose as a symbol of the Infinite Love We Brothers have for you and all mankind. It is this Infinite Love that is the real fabric of life; it is this Love that is the foundation and basis for the coming Age of Spiritual Renaissance. As you begin your presentation, pass this rose on to all who are present, and they too will feel the Love of We Brothers, and this Love will be regenerated as each one shares their own experiences with others." With each word, I felt my energy body bathed in waves of Love energy.

As I awoke in a pillow-full of tears, I felt humbled by and appreciative of the tremendous gift of love and the invaluable lesson I had just received. I knew that Uriel was helping me to overcome my fear of public speaking which still lingered in my consciousness, and to be attuned to the Unarius Brothers as I gave the presentation. I realized what a great opportunity I was being given to turn around my opposition to the Light by serving as a speaker, to help others to know of the reality of spirit and the progressive evolutionary purpose of mankind, rather than lead people astray with the lies, deception which augmented the egocentric lifestyles I promoted in the past. That afternoon, as I began the presentation, I shared my experience with Uriel on the Inner. As I reached out to present the red rose from Uriel to the audience, I felt the overwhelming Love of Uriel envelop me again, and I knew her Love was radiating out to each person attending the Conclave.

Through this contact with Uriel and the Inner, and the sharing of this experience with others, I experienced the great joy of giving and of serving as a Light Bearer. I realized that this is something I must learn to keep uppermost in consciousness throughout each day.

Many wonderful experiences contributed to the positive nature of the Conclave, the release of the 33 white doves, the communication from Uriel, and the various presentations. Yet the experience which, more than any other, left me with a feeling of unity and spiritual purpose as one small facet of a master plan to reawaken mankind to the reality of Spirit and to life on other worlds was the Parade of the Flags of the Interplanetary Confederation, held for the first time at the future landing site. As Marian and I marched at the side of the Space-Cad, leading the flag carriers, it was as though that future day had arrived, the 33 starships had actually landed and the polarities of the 33 worlds were being presented to the world. I felt the excitement of the new, positive changes which lie ahead for the people of Earth.

Yet, as all energy has its positive and negative component, the two-day Conclave of Light was the forum to turn around a tremendously negative past lifetime during the cycle of Isis and Osiris. I realized that I was one of the priests who had opposed Isis and Osiris and rejected their teachings. I took part in their brutal murder, all for the sake of preserving my ego and not letting go of the power and control I held over other people. Despite the transcendence I felt during the presentation, later on I felt like such a phony, like an evangelical priest who had sold a pack of lies to his parishioners by convincing them that the teachings of Isis and Osiris were wrong and that they must not follow them. Through the use of drugs and hypnotic techniques, I sought to manipulate and control the people. I realized that after the murder of Isis and Osiris, I felt such guilt for what I had done, I tried to bury those feelings and disguise who and what I was by running away and taking on a new identity, hoping to forget the horror and deceit I caused. I also took part in getting rid of Seth, whom I both feared and resented; I was a rebel, acting through my own self-righteous belief that I knew best, no matter what anyone else said.

Many other experiences in the planning and preparation for the Conclave replayed the long-forgotten memories of this past. While practicing for the Parade of the Flags, I became reattuned to the celebration of the departure of Isis and Osiris, where they and their entourage paraded between two lines of people, unaware of the brutality that awaited them. I felt great guilt, for I knew I had been one who stood among the crowd and participated in this despicable act of violence. Once I recognized this, marching along side the Space-Cad became a very exciting and meaningful preparation for the Conclave. I also was to help create an inflatable starship balloon (which was never constructed); my present motivation was from past guilt, for promoting the belief that there were no such things as starships and life on other worlds.

Overall, this 13th Annual Conclave of Light provided me with many valuable experiences upon which to grow, both personally and spiritually. I have gained a new appreciation for the Unarius Mission and dedication to my own spiritual growth.

Gary Kainz

Panic was gripping me like never before. I reflected on how I'd nearly been shot to death by police officers while being arrested for drug possession. I had felt the humiliation of public embarrassment, the pain I'd put my family through, the trauma of trial and my 18 month imprisonment, the added trauma of the modern day inquisition, the Grand Jury. But this was worse!

I had moved to El Cajon several months ago to become more involved at the New World Teaching Center and to address my negative past. A few days ago in conversation with Antares, we had discussed the possibility that I would speak at the upcoming Interplanetary Conclave of Light Celebration, that I would open the event with a presentation on the book *Preparation for the Landing*. I had felt comfortable with that, even excited, but now, a few days later, the reality of what that really meant was sinking in. This was not going to be a simple book report. I was being asked to represent the Brothers, to be an open conduit for them, and I just couldn't see how I could do that.

I immediately started taking what I thought was an objective look at my life. I really enjoyed the classes at the Center, but the rest of my life seemed so unintegrated. The thought that I was struggling at my work came through, but that's watered down. I hated my job! My social life the past couple of years hadn't been that memorable, but here in El Cajon I had none!

As a cockroach wandered across the kitchen counter, my mind drifted back to my apartment in Malibu where I'd lived the past two years, high on a bluff overlooking the Pacific Ocean, and where I'd rediscovered nature, hiking in the canyons of the Santa Monica Mountains. A letter from my previous employer inviting me back to work in Beverly Hills was setting on the kitchen table. A powerful urge to rent a U-haul truck came through me, and then I thought, "No, I'll just pack the car with what I can and move back to Los Angeles." My mind was swirling in confusion.

I had been a home study student for nearly ten years. I know intuitively that I'd worked many lifetimes to get to this point in my evolution where I could address my past and bring my electronic energy body into a better balance. And now, after only having been here a few months, I was thinking about moving back! No! I wouldn't do that! But I had to call Antares. To be a presenter in my present state of consciousness would be totally hypocritical, and I backed down. I knew the pressure I was feeling was guilt, great guilt from having participated in the plot to assassinate Osiris and Isis and their followers. But I needed a clearer picture, something more specific. My future was hanging in the balance here, and so with renewed determination I began to objectify, to look at the clues.

At work I saw myself in the owners of the company, as greedy number crunchers who created a highly competitive, hostile working atmosphere, controlling their employees through fear. I saw myself in my immediate supervisor, a shallow, insensitive, unintelligent lady, the perfect "dumb blonde." I realized that in this past I had absolutely no concern for the feelings and emotions of others. As a student-follower of Osiris and Isis, I was aware of a developing opposition to their leadership and, although I listened attentively, I remained loyal, at first. As the power of the opposition grew, I became concerned about my position and felt my life might be in danger. I began to look at my situation from a different perspective.

Many of my fellow students were progressing, developing their creative abilities. I felt inferior and resented the fact that Isis paid little or no attention to me. I began to cooperate with the opposition, at first tentatively, writing and distributing literature. On the surface I continued to be the loyal student, but my resentful, fiercely competitive nature had taken over my consciousness. I now become completely immersed with the opposition.

As I worked through this, it was easy to see why I felt like a hypocrite. I began to feel like a student again and began looking at the upcoming celebration with a new attitude. Maybe I could participate in some way. A couple of days later Antares asked me to be the Master of Ceremonies, and I accepted. I knew I'd struggle with this, but I felt I could see it through. Along the way I caught more glimpses of my participation in this horrible past with my involvement in drugging the water and in stealing phasers from the temple.

On Saturday morning, as I stood in front of the audience preparing to introduce everyone to the celebration, my guilt once again became apparent. I was very nervous, but humble. I felt the love of those in the audience, and I felt the love of the Brothers. As the day went on I began to relax. I had prepared myself to introduce the presenters, but words were coming into my mind that were not part of that preparation. This caused me to stumble occasionally in my introductions, but I was learning to trust myself, that indeed I was somewhat open to the Brothers.

By Sunday I was feeling much more comfortable and relaxed, and I felt I was experiencing something very, very special, something I struggle to find words for. Tears welled up in my eyes several times. Despite my opposition to Spirit I could feel the Love of the Brothers, that they still accepted me. My guilt was my own, they did not hold it against me. The magnanimity of what was happening began to seep into my mind. We were all working together welcoming the Space Brothers back! What a tremendous event that will be for our planet Earth. The thought came through that residents of the planets of the Interplanetary

Confederation, and perhaps residents of countless other planets, were participating, watching, and encouraging us. I felt so, so grateful for having had the opportunity to participate in this incredible event, to be part of a welcoming group of people expressing so unselfishly their love!

In the ensuing days, I realized how much work I have to do, how much I have to learn, that I need to be much more dedicated to my studies, less selfish with my consciousness.

I can find words, however, to relate how my life has changed in the past month. At work I am seeing everyone with new eyes, as spiritual beings. I received a promotion and a raise that I didn't have to ask for. This is the result of the real change, the change in my consciousness, my attitude toward life. Instead of hating my job, I've now found some joy in it. I'm taking a keener interest in the people I meet, their problems, their needs. My attitude is a little lighter, my smile a little quicker. I'm meeting life's challenges with a little more joie-de-vivre. I can even relate to that cockroach on the kitchen counter, that it has its place somewhere in the Grand Design.

With this I express my sincerest and deepest gratitude to the Brothers, to Raphiel and Uriel, to Antares, and to my fellow students. Thank You.

Jack Anton Appel

Antares, I want to tell you about the experience I had during the Interplanetary Conclave of Light. I was in a very negative state of mind in the months leading up to the Conclave weekend, and I hadn't been aware of the extent of this opposition. Watching the Conclave procession had uplifted me for the first time since the planning of the event began; I was happy to be a part of the Mission.

While listening to Carlos Redhead talk on Sunday, I was struck with the sincerity of his words and the reality of the Mission. I became very remorseful that I had not been able to see the positive nature of my involvement with the audio department or any other facet of Unarius. This problem has plagued me for many years. My audio work in preparation for the Conclave of Light was done because I felt like I had to do it, not because I wanted to give freely of myself.

The uplifted state of mind I experienced as a result of the beautiful Conclave of Light enabled me to look back at my thoughts and emotions over the previous months and realize that I had been very opposed to the Mission. I was feeling such love and such a change in my state of mind that I was able to see that my opposition was a much bigger problem than I had thought. I began to question myself. How could I feel this way about such a beautiful Science of Love and healing? I was finally able to see that my involvement in the audio work for the Conclave was a great opportunity and something that I was very happy to be a part of.

Immediately, upon arriving home after such a wonderful experience, I again asked myself why I had become so opposed to Uriel and why had I been unaware of this opposition that was such a huge block. I felt prompted to sit down in front of the microphone and to ask Uriel for help. I was mentally open for it; I knew I was in trouble. This is what transpired.

Jack: "Hello Brothers—Uriel. It is with great feeling that I contact you. This feeling is due to the upliftment I experienced over the last several days at the Interplanetary Conclave of Light. It was a wonderful experience for me, an eye opener, as I was unable to see anything positive in the work that I was putting out in the weeks preceding the event. I have learned, because of this uplifted feeling, that I have not really accepted or realized the level of my negative state of mind prior to this weekend. I was questioning how I could oppose such a wonderful thing and how I could not see that taking part in the procession and the operation of the audio equipment, was a wonderful opportunity. In fact, I saw it as nothing but labor, and not a labor of love.

"As I received information while writing in my journal last evening, I was given help with my opposition to you, Uriel, and the many Brothers. It was due to the fact that I had constructed for myself a mental barrier authority. I had been a department head and as a result was more accustomed to giving the orders rather than taking them as a pawn does in the Orion network—just relay the orders down from up above. But the particular position I had was such that I only dealt with a few people who had a higher position, so I felt I was superior.

"I would like to continue on as you stated last evening to receive more information. I am very ready to accept it because the realization of my opposition has deeply, deeply moved me and I am very remorseful. I wish to not have this opposition. I have experienced such wonderful feelings of being part of the arrival of the Brothers and part of the Interplanetary Confederation that I do not ever want to be an opposing force."

Brothers: "Dear one, you have forgotten that we are always right here, and you need not ask for contact for we are always here? Just open up and we are there, and it is no different now. It has never been any different. We wish nothing but to help.

"Yes, as you have stated from previous contact with us, this is true that you were in this sort of position although one is never in a total position of leadership in the Orion framework as there were many checks and balances. Unbeknownst to yourself you were watched much more closely than you were allowed to know. In this position you did feel a superiority, and it was built by you over the many lifetimes, the many years of pursuing this goal of moving up the ladder. You were told that your job was very important and very special. Many lifetimes you built up this exaggerated ego thinking that you were a vital link in the Orion government.

"So naturally, when Dalos came and visited Tyron, there was a tremendous rifting in your mind, a tumultuous aggravation. How could this Being tell you what is good and what is better, when you know it already? There are no teachers better than the ones you knew. This was your mindset. You were not open. You saw Dalos as a threat—a method of eliminating jobs such as yours, which were based on distrust and control, for now, if people were allowed to act freely and think for themselves, what would you have done? You could not perceive anything positive. You did not agree that this could be done. You felt the people were far too foolish and helpless on their own.

"There was no other recourse, and what needed to be done was to get this man Dalos into the research labs and determine what means he was using to entice people with the electronics. The Orionites could not comprehend that Dalos was of an immense proportion, mentally speaking. His small physical stature, and we mean small relatively speaking in reference to the psychic mind of Uriel, was all that could be comprehended by yourself and the group of Orionites that had the very fortunate experience for their evolution of meeting this enlightened man.

"Your resentment came about when you saw no success in the attempts to silence Dalos, and in fact, you disagreed with what Dalos said so emphatically. You were totally convinced that this man was a total, as you would say on your earth world, raving lunatic. You were confused as to how such a man with such an unstable mind could possibly have arrived on such a spaceship with such modern electronics and other items. But the justification process never ceased in your mind, and it was assumed that the ship was functioning by a robot and that this man could merely come and go as he pleased due to the fact that the robot was programmed to do so, to allow Dalos to do this, and to recognize Dalos' presence and open the door and let him in.

"The use of implants was quite popular in Orion, detrimentally so, but regardless popular. So this is what was assumed to be in the mind of Dalos, an implant, a computer link relaying messages back to a much stronger transmission source where the Pleiadean scientists had learned, so you thought, to manipulate the Orionites' minds in such a way to make them disregard their programming so that they could not be happy. They knew inwardly they were being touched by something of a high frequency. It stirred their minds; it stirred them out of their complacency. This was the necessary element to begin to break their minds free from the controls of Orion.

"This success angered you. Seeing this man gain the trust of Tyrantus much more than yourself caused a tremendous jealousy; it was a jealousy that has not subsided. Onward, down through the many lifetimes that Uriel has come to this world, you have been jealous because they have always been in a position of what you thought was power, but they were really here to help, as you well know. They were not here to control. Uriel is not a controlling force, but a kind, benevolent, and loving being. There could be no other way that this being could express. You have felt this. We have all been touched by this and it is indeed fortunate that you have been able to feel this over this several day long event of a momentous proportion that has occurred on your Earth planet, for the bringing of the notion that our Brothers will be landing is a wonderful one.

"But the true benefit of this meeting is, and by meeting I mean the Interplanetary Confederation of Light, the true benefit is gained by the working out of the students. Media representation is a tiny percentage of what is really happening to get the word of the landing out. The working out of the resentments towards the Brothers is tantamount to the preparation of the earth peoples, psychically, and the many peoples in the astral linked up to them. This is where the true healing is occurring and this will allow 2001 to be the most wonderful event of the millennium. Not all will think this way. There will be those, that you have well surmised, who will wish to hide their heads in the sands much like the ostrich, but yet the wind still blows their feathers around.

"So with this we bid you a wonderful life and know that with this information you will be free from this block that has plagued you.

"This resentment that we spoke of was violent in the Isis and Osiris era. You felt that you should be a leader as you felt that you were superior to all other leaders that you were viewing. Thus you had resentment towards all leaders and did not really trust any one of them. Your attitude is and was the reason you were demoted, or more correctly cast out of one sect. You were not cooperative; you did not serve well, it was deemed. There were some who you would have gone with, but that is enough. And let us not digress and dwell on this.

The future is yours. We Brothers know this to be true and as I have said: The future is progressive and positive. Believest thou this!"

Jack: I was overcome with joy during the last two sentences. I felt Spirit as I have never before. There has been a wonderful change in my life due to the help of Uriel and I am grateful. Words cannot explain it for me, but it feels wonderful. Peace of mind, compassion, and love are new feelings for me that make me feel very happy to be taking part in Unarius. It has left an indelible mark on me. Thank you.

Betty Wilburn

In this cycle of Isis and Osiris, and as the Conclave of Light Celebration approached, I became very negative. I did not want to participate in the flag ceremony. My opposition was very strong. One great reaction occurred when I was being informed that the flag ceremony was being held in Jamul. This tuned me in to my dislike for the desert and to my fear of the heat.

I wanted to avoid Antares because of my guilt and fear of being exposed as a fraud, and as one against Seth. Notwithstanding my past, I knew all these feelings of opposition must have been from the Isis and Osiris cycle.

This past was over-powering, I wanted to escape, yet I was given an opportunity to participate in a positive way. As I walked down the road during the ceremony, I tuned to Uriel and remembered what Barbara Jane had said, "Uriel gave her Love with the Rose." With this thought, I could feel Uriel's Love during the ceremony.

Gail Orman

I just finished re-reading my notes from the Conclave, and I felt that power and frequency all over again.

First, let me say that, for me, since I have been in Unarius, this was the strongest I ever felt the energies. It seemed as though a strong energy beam was pulsating into the middle of my forehead when I would focus on the celebration and on what it meant to myself and to mankind.

I was excited about coming out to California; even in getting ready for the trip, I could feel the power and could see spirit working.

On my way to the airport in Charlotte, North Carolina, I stopped by the body shop. One of the employees, who is really very negative towards Unarius, started asking me questions, and I was able, with the help of the Brothers, to clear up a lot of misinformation and misconceptions he had about Unarius. When we finished talking, he admitted that he thought there was life on other planets and said he hoped I had a good trip. This was very unlike him.

Then, on the plane going out, I sat next to an elderly lady who was going to San Diego to visit her son. As we settled into the flight, I got out my Tesla book and started to read about the planet that I was representing. I was really enjoying it. About half way through the flight, she asked me what I was reading. I told her I was reading about life on other planets. She said, "Somebody has a good imagination, don't they?" I just smiled back and told her it was all fact—not fiction! Well, to make a long story short, she wanted me to write down the name of the book and where she could get a copy. All I did was read the book. I never tried to tell her anything about Unarius. This was a good example to me, that by raising my own consciousness, I automatically effect everyone around me.

I arrived Thursday night and right away was involved in a reliving. I went to the Center to help put crystals in the new starship pins. When I first saw them, I didn't think they were as pretty as the ones we had before. I thought the gray background looked kind of military, but the shape of them looked more authentic. By the time the night was over, I was agreeing with everyone else that they were beautiful.

Well, almost every morning while I was there I awoke with a dull headache and felt very blocked off. I know this was the feedback from the Steelon cycle when I implanted crystals that would control people on other planets and make zombies of them, and really blocking them from the Light. I know too that this past has a lot to do with why I am so blocked off from electronics today.

Another reliving I had while I was out there was, of course, the Isis and Osiris cycle. I recently started taking a natural vitamin supplement which is supposed to make you more energetic, etc. May wanted some, so I ordered some for her. I was reliving dispensing the drugs that would make everyone crazy enough to commit such a heinous crime. I had a rapport with Samantha when we rode to the landing site and with her after the celebration. We were going back to the landing site to help clean up, and I think we were working together to help dispense the drugs.

Another part of the Steelon cycle came in while at the landing site. Gary and Samantha went down the mountain to bring us some food, and Becky and I were left there by ourselves. I felt like we were guarding the spoils that we had looted from the planet. I know I have stolen from others a lot in the past, and now I am on the other end of that sine wave because I have a constant struggle with finances and with trying to make ends meet. I know that will improve as I work out my past in this way.

So, in retrospect, I learned a lot about myself during the Interplanetary Conclave of Light Celebration, and I'm sure there were other relivings that went on that I haven't yet recognized.

What I learned, or I should say what I became more deeply aware of, is that my consciousness affects everybody. I think I catch it a little quicker now, when I am negative, and I turn it around. The second thing, which made a deep impression on me, is how important it is to be a part of these celebrations, and to get involved. So I am savings my pennies in order to make the trip to California in February. The last but not the least of my deeper awarenesses is that the best way to help my loved ones and all of mankind is by changing myself, which comes about by learning more about energy.

Well, Antares, I thought I was through, but I just thought of a reliving I had with you while I was in El Cajon. Do you remember when we were all at the landing site, and you and Dan were sitting at the table? I asked you if I could take your picture. You said something like, "Just don't show it to anyone." When I said I was going to put it on the front page of the newspaper, you replied, "Then everybody will be able to find me." Then I told you, "That was the whole idea!" I felt I was reliving exposing you during the Isis cycle, just before you were killed.

I am very thankful to the Brothers for all of these recognitions of the past. So, during this Thanksgiving season I would like to say to you that I am very thankful that I am a Unariun and that I have this wonderful opportunity to do my small part in bringing in the new Spiritual Age. And as Uriel so aptly put it, "It is an exciting time, is it not!"

Love and Light to you, Antares, and to all my brothers and sisters in El Cajon.

Bruce Wilson Robinson

The 13th Annual Interplanetary Conclave of Light pulled me away for a moment to see a different reality of life.

In the weeks of preparing for this event, I did not give a lot of energy and support to the Conclave as I have in the past years. This year, as I entered the Unarius Center, I felt as an outsider looking in on a group of people who believed in the coming of spaceships in the year 2001. I could see and feel the unity and commitment to the mission and to the events of the day. I could see the joy and happiness in the eyes of the people all around me. I felt embarrassed that I had so many doubts about the landing and my personal mission.

My conscious reason was that I have been feeling that my life is slipping away and I am not taking the best path. In this limbo of fear and worry, I find I have taken no action and have been falling further behind. I see this reflected to me everywhere, yet after each speaker I was pulled away from these doubts into a beam of love. I felt at one with the universe, and there were no problems without answers. I felt confident, secure, and loved, ready to take the challenges of the day.

I could not tell you what words were spoken that pulled me out of my dark mentality; all I knew was that I felt worthy. I could look at my problems from a perspective high above and see why I was going through these emotional trials, as I felt the presence of my own higher self with me again. I could feel the understanding and love as my higher self spoke softly into my mind, "You have lost all faith in yourself."

As I looked inside myself, I could feel the shame of my

actions. All I wanted to do was run and hide so I didn't have to deal with any responsibility. I could see these thoughts guiding me throughout the past three years or more. Little by little I stopped trusting in myself and started thinking with my conscious mind. "I know best. I can guide myself to a better future. I know what I need."

This is the problem. I stopped trusting in spirit; I was looking at all the people around me, who were feeling left behind and were not taking the fruit of life, yet that is exactly what I was doing. I could see that I needed to go through these experiences so I could see the reality of my situation.

I know I have lost a lot of ground in this search for myself in all the wrong places. However, going through these experiences has helped me feel where I am in the universe. I also can draw on these experiences as I am tempted throughout my life not to follow my inner self. It has been very hard for me to face the truth about myself, even after the Conclave of Light. I know what I must do, but it is hard to start again.

Mark Levenson

To write about the 13th Annual Interplanetary Conclave weekend and my experience with it is very difficult. I have had a strong resistance towards putting into words my feelings as they relate to the celebration. This resistance is the Battle of Armageddon that I have been fighting and have lost through many lifetimes. I felt like a fake throughout the weekend and did not feel a part of the Mission. Yes, I did take part in the flag procession and a few other aspects, but nonetheless I felt the pull of a material consciousness.

It is difficult for me to give of myself without a motive of receiving some sort of recognition. I have been totally immersed, from Orion to the present, in a selfish consciousness that I would very much like to change.

Yes, I did experience some uplifting moments throughout the two days. I felt a beautiful transcendency as the music played during the Parade of the Flags and the dove release, as well as through other various presentations.

This 13th Annual Celebration has brought out many feelings and thoughts within myself. I wish to begin to break down the false barriers of a material configuration and try to conceive what it means to "Seek the Father Within." I have at times felt the overpowering influence of the Brothers and have received help when my channel was open. But these times are too few, and to far between. I am compelled to continue in pursuit of breaking down my walls of fear and ignorance so that I may "come out" and not be afraid to stand for spirit. I wish to thank the Brothers for this opportunity to see myself, as I could not do so in any other way.

Barbara Jarad

The Isis and Osiris cycle has, without a doubt, been the longest in duration and has covered more troubled areas of my present life than any other cycle I have been through.

It started about a year ago with the addition of a new member to our choral group. I was glad, at first, to see another alto in our group but, as soon as she started asking for special attention and help, things changed. I felt great competition with her, and as the months passed and others of the group started extolling her virtues, I started to feel an awful feeling of hatred toward her. This shocked me, and I tried to get to the bottom of the reliving but, try as I may, I could not seem to get to the cause of the problem. In my utter frustration, I called the music director and resigned from the group. Later, I changed my mind because of some counseling I received from our Director, Antares.

I knew it was getting really serious, but I didn't realize, until cautioned by Antares, that I could end up leaving the Unarius School if I severed my tie with the choral group. Of course, I kept digging and waiting for some clue which would bring the understanding I needed. This came when a situation surfaced which revealed that a couple of students, who were themselves psychically leaving the Unarius Center, entered into a whispering campaign against Antares and later provided spurious information to the whole student group.

I could see my complicity in the criticism against him and my lack of participation in the preparations for the up-and-coming Interplanetary Conclave of Light Celebration. I was just frozen with hatred, resentment, and guilt. I couldn't seem to get into the activities, as I had separated myself through my lower-frequency thoughts.

Finally, help was needed on a project at the Lighthouse. I started to work there on a daily basis to complete the project. It was there that the clues I was looking for emerged. I was reliving disposing of Isis and Osiris' belongings after their murders and, as a dutiful son taking orders from his father, I was dismantling the Temple. It was then that I realized that Seth had been my father, and I was, in fact, an unloved son. Because of our past with each other, there was no love and many regrettable deeds ensued that produced great guilt in me towards him. The guilt caused me to become very ill-at-ease around him and I could not express myself intelligently. I had never before been able to accept these guilts because he, Antares, always seemed to have the upper hand, and I always felt so powerless. However, I was able to realize that I had been involved in the conspiracy to kill him.

This enabled me to see myself as an unloving and abusive parent who put career first and neglected, and sometimes even abandoned, my whole family. I came into cycle with a student from North Carolina who came to stay with me. There was a guilt towards him. It also answered a question I had as to why I incarnated, in this lifetime, into a situation where I was an abused child. I could, only then, understand my choice much more clearly and realize that my higher self and my Recording Angels had selected the most pressing problem area for me to work on in this incarnation, and hence be able to move foreward in my progressive evolution. It also was great to realize that there are no mistakes!

I was able, through this understanding, to feel the remorse for all those whose lives I had made so miserable and to extend the love and compassion of Uriel towards all involved, including myself, and a great healing transpired.

I kept feeling that after the murder of Isis and Osiris, in

which I took part, that promises were broken. I lost my position and privilege and had to leave the city. The pieces were coming together, and it now all made sense.

My father, Seth, appointed another person to my position and simply demoted me. Because of this, I suffered a general lack of respect from my former colleagues and great humiliation. Finally, several people wanted to get rid of me and accused me falsely of something I didn't do. I was banished from the city.

This was actually relived on several occasions by me, and I re-experienced the same emotions that I must have felt in that life. I knew that this was the reason I had felt that students wanted to get rid of me when I first came to Unarius, and for many years afterwards. I also recognized why I had hated this new member of our choral group so much, and why I felt so much competition with her. She was my replacement in that past! I now feel respect for this soul's efforts to become a participating part of our choral group, and I no longer feel those past negative emotions connected with that lifetime. I can now welcome her and want to psychically work closer with her to blend our voices in harmony with each other.

I turned on my father, Seth, and joined the conspiracy to kill him, which we did. Those are the kind of acts toward each other that constitute our difficulties. With that realization, however, I could appreciate Antares as our present spiritual leader and stop looking to him for approval, as a child to a parent. Now, because that condition was exposed and rectified, the energy between us has started to change.

Much was boiling beneath the surface, as one can readily surmise, and the Interplanetary Conclave of Light Celebration found me locked in a maze of negative emotions. However, on the first of our two-day event, I was touched by a Love so dynamic that it melted my frozen state of mind. For the first time in my life I was truly transcended and was out of my body for a week afterwards. It was a positive turning point in my experience, and I will never be the same.

The thing that made our celebration so dynamic this year was that there were several "firsts" incorporated within it. It was the first time we had ever prepared and used the landing site for our ceremony. Students, who had never before been the featured speakers, stepped up as channels for the Brotherhood. The scheduled topics were presented with a professionalism never before achieved. No one present had ever witnessed a celebration with this integration before, and therefore they were almost "propelled out" of their bodies. The frequency was of the highest caliber.

As for myself, the memory of my transcended state was the experience I needed to finally convince me that life on the higher dimensions is definitely preferable. Now I try to tune-in to a higher frequency in my daily life every moment possible.

My whole slant on life has changed, and I find myself calm and happy in the face of adversity. I am experiencing a lightness that I have yearned for all my life. I'm truly laughing these days. There is also very little fear left as a residue, and I am speaking my mind honestly, which is a complete reversal of what I felt before. I no longer am fearful of exposing myself.

I know that this new cycle is positive because of my own results. I hear that others are doing the same, and I believe that the work that each and every student has done on their own is now paying off in terms of strengthened links in the spiritual chain amongst our student body.

There's a whole new ball game in play, with coaching from above, and we can look forward to a new season of power-packed expression. The by-words are "together, we are better."

Nanette Breault

During the preparation for the Interplanetary Conclave, while most people were preparing the land for the day of the celebration, which I felt incapable of doing physically, I was editing the transcription of class sessions on the cycle of Isis and Osiris and gathering these classes to begin a book on the Isis and Osiris Cycle.

No matter what we are doing, we are repeating our past, and that to me represents gathering information against Isis and Osiris to be given to other people involved to prepare for the murder of these two Spiritual Beings.

I relived hearing their screams of death one day while working on one of the class sessions. My daughter was in the other room and was emptying a bottle of shampoo into another bottle. (At the time, I had no idea that this is what she was doing) Upon hearing that noise, which sounded like somebody was screaming, I became so frightened that my whole body was vibrating and I could not continue my work. I sat quietly and began asking inwardly, "What is this? What did it tune me into? Why am I experiencing this great fear?" Immediately the answer came. "Those were the screams of Isis and Osiris. If you could have experienced beforehand the pain and suffering of your murder victims, you would have never, never been able to take part in this insane murder." As I was hearing this, tears of remorse began to fall. I cried very hard, and as I am re-attuning to it now, I again cannot hold back my tears.

After the massacre, I wanted my reward that we were all promised by Seth, if we took part, but when I did not get my reward, a great anger came over me and I vowed to get rid of Seth (who is the present Antares). I joined forces with Lianne and Joseph and plotted to kill Seth. An assassin was hired to kill him, which was Richard, a present Unariun student.

I relived my part when Richard walked into the Center upon his arrival from Atlanta. As soon as I saw him a great fear came upon me; my heart began to beat wildly and I began to feel nauseated. I hurried to tell Carol of his arrival. Right at this point a picture flashed in front of me—I was announcing that the assassin had arrived, and it was now time to get rid of Seth. My great fear of seeing Richard was actually my guilt in taking part in another murder.

My guilt in that past of having taken part in so many murders was so great that I could not face what I had done; it was too much for me to bear. As a way to forget, I joined the sex cults and buried myself in sex, believing that the joy of sex would erase all the atrocities that I had done, but this activity wasn't enough; my guilt became stronger and stronger to the point that I committed suicide.

During the preparation for the Interplanetary Conclave Celebration, as I relived these very negative pasts in the present lifetime, I felt many times that I would lose my sanity, (like I had done in that lifetime). I experienced all the anger, resentment, and hatred that I had experienced in that lifetime. I had several dreams of Lianne and Joseph, and frankly that worried me. I began to wonder if they would be successful in taking me over on their negative side of life, like they had done in that past. (These two individuals were unable to face their past and left the Unarius Science in the present.) I fought them in my dreams and told them to leave, that they were not allowed to come back. But for me to get completely free of their negative influences is to accept that I had joined them in these murders. While preparing for the event, I had never come so close to losing all the progress that I had accumulated so far in overcoming my negative self.

As the day of the celebration approached, I was

concerned that I would not be able to appreciate the event, as I had in previous times. So when Saturday came I was very surprised that I was able to rise above my negations. As I listened to Antares speak about "The Grand Design of Life," I began to rise in consciousness. Then came Marian to speak about the future of our Earth world. Tears began to fall when she began to describe Commander Star's arrival with his spaceship, and I could see Commander Star standing at the top of the stairs, waving to the earth people below who were welcoming him to our earth world.

After Marian finished speaking, and this is very hard for me to understand, I felt as if a thousand years had passed. I felt as if I had always lived in that beautiful state of consciousness. It is very hard to explain. When I looked at my watch, I could not believe that only a few hours had passed. Needless to say, the rest of the afternoon was very beautiful; and when the time came to leave the Center, I didn't want to leave.

The next day, Sunday, I looked forward with much anticipation to the time of the Interplanetary Flag March. Upon arriving at the landing site, I proudly picked up the flag of the Planet Luminus and began tuning in to its leader, Lumins. As we began marching to the beautiful transcending music, I began visualizing that this was the day of the real landing. As I listened to this beautiful music, I could see in my mind the thirty-three spaceships aligning themselves to descend. With each beat of the music one spaceship would land, and with the next beat, the next one would land on top of the other. As I watched this scene in my mind's eyes, tears were flowing and I wondered if perchance there would be a parade such as this one on the day of the Landing?

As the thirty-three representatives of each planet approached in a single line, stopping for a moment for the announcement of their planet, to me this represented the announcement of each spaceship as it touched our Earth.

Watching the thirty-three white doves of peace rise up to the sky and circle around and around, I couldn't stop thinking that they seemed to be so proud of the part they are playing in this momentous event.

These two days were the most beautiful days of my life, nothing on Earth can be more beautiful than to feel this high, transcending feeling. I wish that the whole world could feel what I felt, and, if they could, their whole consciousness would change, as did mine. I am no longer the person I was before this event. I no longer feel the heaviness that I felt prior to these two days. I have now regained my attunement to my Spiritual Teacher, Uriel, and I am so very happy. Thank you, Uriel, with all my heart and soul.

David Reynolds

The 13th Annual Interplanetary Conclave of Light Celebration was the best yet! It was an honor and a tremendous privilege to have been given an opportunity to speak on behalf of the Advanced Intellects who are the designers of the Interplanetary Confederation, a cosmic Brotherhood whose grand design will finally be made public on this world in 2001 in a mission for peace and progressive development. In addition to speaking about the Atlantean-Pleiadean connection, I appreciated the opportunity to work with Marian Keymas and Dan Smith in the workshop held on Sunday.

In the planning stages, we became aware of our efforts to thwart the landing of the Space Brothers, via spacecraft, during a previous time in Egypt. During this cycle, known as the Isis and Osiris cycle, these advanced spiritual teachers escaped from the sinking continent of Atlantis to re-seed the colony in Egypt. Almost everyone, including myself, noticed subconscious opposition to the preparations we were carrying out for the October symposium. Headaches and lethargy were some of the symptoms being dealt with and openly discussed in our past-life therapy meetings; but everyone kept to their moral obligation to objectify and to recognize their relivings from this past-life influence. Everyone had their part to play and we all worked together harmoniously, each helping the other wherever the need arose. Many were the lessons learned, individually and as a group! Never had the group expressed so positively, in a unified consciousness, since we began to celebrate the future landing of our Space Brothers.

In one of the planning meetings, a map of the landing area in Jamul was roughly sketched on the chalkboard. I had a psychic awareness that this was a reliving of sketching out the landing area in Egypt, at the time of Isis and Osiris. But, in that long ago time, my classmates and I were making plans to thwart the landing of the Space Brothers who were on a positive mission. Had I, at that time, known the principles of the continuity of life, and had I conceived how this murderous act would severely hold back the progressive development of future generations, I would not have given in to the forces of criticism, fear, resentment, or envy.

In the present, I felt glad and thankful that I was no longer a part of the negative forces. During the next several class sessions, we were able to recognize the inner opposition we had set in motion at that time in Egypt, and we were able to objectify this opposition in our past-life therapy sessions, thus strengthening our resolve to work for the positive forces.

It was realized, in our group meetings, that to have carried out such a demonic murderous plot, everyone who was a part of the negative reactionary group had been drugged in some manner; their minds, being held in some stupor, they were more easily controlled and manipulated. One of the ways that drugs were continuously introduced was through the water supply. At the landing site in Jamul, there was a struggle to get the pump and generator operational so as to provide water and electricity.

Meanwhile, I was undergoing a parallel workout with getting the Tesla Power Tower mockup in the Unarius Center operational in time for the celebration. Over the years, the water in it had become permeated with algae so that when the pump was turned on the water became cloudy. The column lights also had burned out. Several chemical treatments were tried, but none were successful in cleansing the tower of its pollutants. With the realization that the murky water was a psychic outpicturing, or a regeneration of our past negative expressions carried into the present, we were able to restore the tower to its original crystal clarity.

There were several planning meetings involving those students who were to be presenters for the symposium. During one meeting I felt "talked down to" or "talked to in a condescending manner," and because of the resultant ego deflation, I felt anger and resentment to the channel, Antares. He was influenced psychically by our teacher Uriel to say things in a manner which would bring to the surface conscious mind my hidden resentment to spirit and to the truth of myself. I realized I was angry at Uriel, not Antares! This anger was a direct reliving of my negative involvement in opposing the forces of Light. It epitomized the way I reacted to my teachers, Isis and Osiris, and it epitomized my lack of ability to accept an ego deflation. This lack of humility toward my spiritual teachers, in that time in Egypt and in other lifetimes, exemplified my myopic attitude. I thought I was more intelligent than they and believed that I was justified in carrying out extreme savageness against the Lighted ones. This was one of the greatest past-life overcomings I have experienced since becoming a Unariun!

On a positive note, I was able to sit on the front row to take pictures of the flag procession, which was quite beautiful to watch. Psychically, I felt a warm, positive, velvety texture as the procession descended down the hill. I realized this was the high-frequency healing energies being demodulated and brought into our earth plane by the Space Brothers. There was a definite sensing of love in the atmosphere, as well as a strong group togetherness.

The transmission that evening from the Unariun Brotherhood was another high point of the two-day symposium. I appreciated the words of our dear teacher, Uriel, who stated clearly that this was a new beginning for us, individually, as a group, and as a planet. The rose of love from Uriel that was handed-out afterward was certainly more than I expected. The words spoken through the channel were words of encouragement and love, and they touched me greatly.

The next few days, I inwardly sensed the higher energies from the Brothers still regenerating; it seemed like the celebration was still going on. My appreciation for the present director of the Unarius Center, Antares, runs very high, as he overcame direct opposition to this symposium from many diverse sources. He is an excellent role model in helping us strengthen our spiritual legs and overcome our lower reactionary nature.

Margaret Charette

"Dear students of the Light" were Uriel's first words as she welcomed us into the great magnificent Lighted Temple. She spoke of the purpose of this 13th Interplanetary Conclave of Light saying, "We are celebrating the fact that the curtain which has closed planet Earth from other habitable planets is rising!"

Sometimes I have difficulty believing myself to be a student of Light, although I know it is true. On this occasion, seated in a tent, it greatly stretched my imagination to believe that I was in a magnificent lighted temple in the inner worlds. The material curtain was all that I could see at the moment but, as I listened to the words of Uriel, the Power transcended me out of my body and I was in that Lighted Temple!

Earlier in the day, while we flag carriers were waiting to begin marching down the hill, the student, who had planned and directed what we were to do, decided to use guided imagery. Attuned to my past I thought, "She's going to preach again! She's attempting to energize the troops!" So I walked a few steps and turned my gaze towards the distant hills and thought about the future of this polarized property—a university that will be built when the 33 spaceships descend, a university where students will have an opportunity to make the Unarius principles their own, an environment where people will learn by participating in their own positive evolution, where children and adults will learn to monitor their thoughts and catch their negative reactions to persons, places and things. They will learn how to heal themselves mentally and physically as they recognize themselves in the mirror of each other.

The loud marching music suddenly brought me back to

the celebration. I was carrying the flag of planet Idonus, a small planet that had feared technology. The people lived a simple, pleasurable life without much analysis or concern for the future. I relate to both a fear and fascination of technology—especially computers.

The marching music tuned me into military marches and violence, but I also knew that what I was doing was positive and helping to turn around a very negative cycle in Egypt—the murder of our teachers. In the present, I felt transcended and a part of the positive future, but in the past, as a student of Isis and Osiris, I was not sufficiently dedicated and became fearful if I didn't go along with the crowd bent on violence. I didn't have the strength to follow my inner guidance, so I participated in the murders!

Until now, I haven't been able to accept this awful truth. In my first year as a home study student of Unarius, I wrote a note to Uriel in red ink. She wrote back that she saw blood when she first viewed my note to her. Later, when I read in a Unarius book about the students murdering their teachers, Isis and Osiris, in such a brutal manner, I thought to myself, "I hope I wasn't one of them." Just that thought puts me there, and the guilt of not wishing to reveal this thought is proof of my involvement.

Previous to this Conclave celebration, I had recognized and relived lifetimes in Egypt as a scribe-priest who was more interested in maintining his security and position than learning the Truth of Life or helping the people have more fullfilling lives. The impressive temples with their hiero-glyphs, the pyramids and the Sphynx, and the archaelogical and anthropological discoveries of this ancient land have always fascinated me.

When I learned from my Unarius studies that Egypt was once a colony of Atlantis, I felt that I had lived in both civilizations. Just hearing the names of the Spiritual Broth-ers—Isis and Osiris, Hatseptsut, Queen Tiy and Akhena-ton—has always caused me to have 'goose bumps'— proof to me of having known, in some manner, these amazing Leaders. As a beginning student of Spirit, I both admired and was jealous of their intelligence and compassion. I resented the many deflations to my ego, not realizing fully their motivation and teaching methods.

I realize now that when I distanced myself from the group, in present time, I was again attempting to disassociate myself from the murder plan, but I hadn't the strength to go against my peers.

The heavy curtain that has separated me from my teacher, Uriel, now can begin to lift as I become more honest about my evil deeds. I am ashamed that I could turn on the one who has always loved me and is now urging me to be truthful and admit my participation.

Perhaps now the psychic amnesia that I feel will begin to lift and I can recognize and accept my guilty feelings and know where they originated. I have now proven to myself that psychic amnesia is caused by having opposed Brothers of the Light who came to teach about progressive evolution, the continuity of life after death and the reality of Spirit. These teachers live these truths and share what they have learned with all who are open and capable of raising their consciousness to receive.

I did appreciate the opportunity to participate in this 13th Interplanetary Conclave of Light—the raising of the spiritual curtain—the positive future for planet Earth as it becomes the 33rd planet of the Interplanetary Confederation.

The 33 planets and their problems have held a special interest for me. I compiled what I call my "IPC Study Guide." It was a method of study as I read the extensive information in the Unarius books about how problems similar to our own were solved. I have wondered why I went to such effort to collect and organize this information. Recently I have concluded that in Orion I accepted a position to study and collect pertinent information about certain planets that were marked for take-over. I was never told that this was the purpose, but I knew. That's where the push in this lifetime originated and why I was determined to finish my study guide. I have wondered how particular planets are progressing and desire a contact with the various planetary leaders. I know that to have such a mental conversation I need to raise my frequency. This is an evolutionary development, so I will be patient with myself and know that it is part of my positive future.

Accepting my feelings of guilt has helped me to accept my violent opposition to my teachers, Isis and Osiris. By this admission, I am now more firm in my commitment to my progressive development because I understand more clearly my motivations in this Egyptian lifetime. I understand better the student/teacher relationship. I am more willing to accept ego deflations. I am learning not to say "I know," but to be open to new information and to ask questions of myself.

How privileged I am to be a student of Unarius, to observe the million-year plan unfold and to know that the Golden Bell has rung on the Inner Worlds in celebration of the success of the Light Forces over the dark forces. I am determined to continually confront my negative past actions. By doing this, I will raise my frequency to be a better conduit for the Love of the Brothers. The Spiritual Curtain is rising to reveal the positive future that Uriel has always predicted—"The future is positive! I promise you!"

Robert Ellingson

Reflecting back upon my experiences during the Interplanetary Conclave Celebration, I am struck with one blatant element within my psyche. That is the element of resistance. This resistance became evident in my thoughts and attitude toward the celebration. I did have the wish that the event would be unsuccessful and have a low turn out, and my attitude showed signs of criticism toward all that went on.

Seeing these surface elements of negative thoughts and attitudes, I knew there must be some underlying cause in my previous history to explain such surface manifestations.

There was a period during the reign of the Orion empire when I was a starship commander. The nature of our missions were that of destruction and the aggressive takeover of peaceful worlds. Therefore, part of the resistance I have toward the peaceful landing of spaceships here on earth is that it amplifies the guilt of having used my mind in a destructive fashion toward humanity.

I also realized that I carry the attitude that I do not need the help of higher intelligences, that I have a mind and I can solve my own problems. It is evident that this resistance is a by-product of my ego who wants to keep its identity separate from the whole. My ego resists any event that serves to unify mankind in fear that it will lose its sense of importance in the scheme of life.

I have a feeling this is not all the factors involved in my resistance toward the Interplanetary Confederation. But these insights into my past and into my psychological make-up should serve as a start toward getting at the deeper causes.

William Proctor

"Love, Love, Love" are three beautiful words pronounced by Uriel that perfectly fit the 13th Annual Conclave of Light Celebration held October, 1996.

When the preparations began I was excited, but there was a very subtle cloud of resistance within me that was beginning to slow me down. After recognizing it was a reflection of my own past, I knew that it was opposition towards the Light, from the lifetime of Isis and Osiris, where I chose once again to align myself with the negative forces. I saw in a dream where I had struck Osiris from behind, and this was causing the intense back pain I felt only when I would arrive at the land to start working. When I looked at the dream and was able to accept what I had done, honestly, the pain in my back did not return. My own opposition toward Isis and Osiris was my downfall. I had only an interest for power and position. Because of my very selfish nature, I ignored what these two beautiful teachers of spirit truly had to give.

After their murders, I still wasn't satisfied. Hate, resentment, and guilt, then involved me along with the conspiracy to murder Seth. All this added tremendous guilt that eventually drove me to take my own life. I relived this one Monday, after a weekend working at the land. It was really interesting. I felt like I had no consciousness, no rapport with anything around me. I knew I had to resolve this horrible state of mind. When I asked for help from within, a compassionate voice entered my mind, saying, "You're dead." That realization totally brought me back on-line, so to speak. It was an immediate change from a negative state of mind to a positive state of mind, something I had never experienced before.

I began to help, in whatever way I could, to do whatever it took, not seeking a particular position as from the past, but working with others making the work at the land a positive and easy endeavor. Upon accepting my own negative involvement in opposing the Light, it was now my responsibility to become positively involved. The days for opposing the Light were over. Learning to be open to spirit is a reward that opened the door to a beautiful gathering of spirit and a very special experience for myself.

Driving the "Space-Cad" was an energy-packed experience, and I appreciated being a "conduit for spirit"! I felt tremendous love when I looked in the rear view mirror of the "Cad" and saw the smiling faces of the flag carriers. All the Brothers of the thirty-two other worlds were definitely present and accounted for. The trumpeteers were heralding the positive future in store for planet Earth and ringing in the new age of logic and reason for the year 2001. There are truly no words to express it better than, "Love, Love, Love"!!!

It was the place I wanted to be. It is a pathway I am so glad I allowed myself to find. The whole time I was driving down the hill, I felt so much appreciation for Uriel and the Brothers. As a matter of fact, I imagined Uriel riding in the passenger seat, waving to the world! It brought tears to my eyes to see myself as her chauffeur, without the opposition I had in the past. I also asked myself, "How in the world could I have ever gone against such love and understanding that the Brothers give ever so freely? Where have I been??? Dead!!!"

Last, but assuredly not least, was the loving hand of Uriel overshadowing our Brother Antares as he brought in the Ultimate Wisdom of love which was, and still is, the true success of the 13th Annual Conclave of Light! As Uriel spoke through Antares (tears as I type), I could not, and wouldn't want to hold back the tears. They were a magnification of the healing energies engulfing not just the people at the Conclave, but actually (I stopped typing--tears again) the entire Earth!

After the transmission, the love continued with Uriel again coming through Antares as he gave roses to certain individuals present. I was one that was fortunate enough to receive such a glorious gift of spirit. To me, it represented an alignment with spirit I had lost many lifetimes ago. It was a true contact, a one-on-one contact between Uriel and myself. I made a re-commitment to my spiritual teacher I will never break, and to my own spiritual evolution. I will never, ever, break. I truly felt it was a homecoming for me! This beautiful experience will always be with me in days to come. It is a love that continues to build within my soul. I know it is entirely up to me how big this inner flame can get and how bright it shall become in the future.

On that note, I say many infinite thanks to Uriel and to the entire Unarius Brotherhood, of which I am grateful to be a part. Many more thanks to my dear, Brother in Light, Antares, for being the conduit for the Light, which he truly is, that was and still is, that expression of those three words that will forever remain in my consciousness; Love, Love, Love!!!

Frank Garlock

Even though I was aware I was reliving the time of Isis and Osiris in Egypt during the preparations for the 13th Annual Interplanetary Conclave of Light, I had no idea how really important the expanding of this event, to take place both at the Unarius Center in El Cajon and at the Unarius future landing site in Jamul, California, would mean to me.

No coincidence, I became the logistical planning person, as a direct conduit through Antares and my past, to help coordinate, with others, the preparation of the land, to facilitate the parade of the Interplanetary Confederation, lecture explaining the Interplanetary Conclave, catered buffet dinner, a live Cosmic Connection, *The Arrival* film, and concluding with stargazing with telescopes viewing the Milky Way Galaxy.

This involved contracting new electrical service, activating a well for drinking and irrigation water, landscaping, and grading the land for a tent, dining, and buses, and coordinating schedules for work to be done, tools needed and the rental of astro-turf, chairs, tables, tent, sound system, motor home and buses.

The purpose and the success of this event is to alert all humankind to the positive future for planet Earth and to the truth that there is human life on other worlds helping us to become the 33rd planet in the Interplanetary Confederation as part of the evolutionary moving forward of the Milky Way Galaxy.

However, the true prime purpose is my overcoming of my negative past, as well as others so choosing to do so, related to this time of Isis and Osiris. It's in the positive turn-around that progress is made. But first, I have to understand, feel the remorse, and accept the horror of my negative acts, let go and replace them with positive deeds with my greater understanding of the Unarius Mission and my progressive evolution.

Therefore, everything that went wrong, that was delayed, and/or caused me any reaction, were all clues for me to analyze as being from my past. As I realized and accepted the truth about each reaction from my relentless pushing to get the job done, disposing of bodies through the chipper, my emotional outbreak that our temporary generator would not start for a necessary watering cycle for forty-seven oleanders we had just planted along the parade route, (which represented life, human life, Isis and Osiris, and their followers I had no regard for), explains my terrible emotions, which were from the guilt I had.

As we came closer to the date of the Conclave, we finalized the tent size, amount of chairs, tables and turf to arrive and be installed just in time. The rental store decided, because of their work load, to deliver and install a day earlier than planned. This seemed fine to me, but I found myself being pushed and things were not going right. I complained about the gray tape on unmatched green turf, old tape residue on turf, and irregular side panels on tent. I was told; "That's all that is available."

When speaking on the phone with Antares, he noticed a lack of enthusiasm from me. I was down, going further down, and the next morning I avoided the tent. Then I finally sat down in the tent to become completely devastated with the filthy mess, including the red marks representing the bloodshed from the past. As David K., and William came in, I knew I had to get this corrected.

I borrowed William's cell-phone and registered my complaint. I could not keep the connection long enough to resolve the problem. I knew I had to get to a hard-wired phone. David had an emergency page and joined me on the ride down the hill.

Meanwhile, Antares already had sensed the problem and

met us on the road. I explained and stressed the need to get to a hard-wired phone at the 7/11 convenience store to correct this problem.

I spoke with the rental manager, who refused to do anything on the phone. I had to go in face to face to work it out. By this time Antares had driven up and I said, "I have to go in face to face." Antares suggested David go along as a polarity. I said, "Great!"

As David and I traveled to the rental store, we stopped to eat the lunch Antares brought to us. This was an opportunity to calm down and be more prepared to negotiate the corrections. The manager at the rental store was totally in a rage and was not going to do a thing, and if that was not acceptable, they were coming out to remove everything on the eve of our event.

Fortunately, she got interrupted and we backed away. I said to David, "We need to leave and call Antares." Upon doing so, he immediately said; "Go to the yellow pages and line up another rental company." I accepted his direction as from the most high and, with the help of David, the new rental was set.

In the meantime, I found some quiet time to review all that had taken place, to realize how off I was, how negative, how brutal— thoughts of getting rid of Seth, and that I was opposed to the Landing in 2001. I realized the surprise of my life was when I accepted directional help from Antares, as my teacher and Brother of the Light, no longer Seth. This realization came with overwhelming kindness, truly the love of Uriel, which I longed for, was always there.

The contrast from the insatiable dilemma I was in was overwhelming to me. Everyone who came appeared as part of a crew of Angels to help remove the old, making room for the new. It didn't stop. That's true love! Therefore, I was able to carry the flag of planet Delna believing their overcoming they had with materialism and selfishness, with the help of Uriel, and feeling and seeing it happening within myself as I continued in the parade, hearing the proclamation as never before, the thrill of the releasing of 33 doves, and on to the tent, with this new consciousness and sense of well-being, freed from that horrible past, to hear with new ears more words on the Interplanetary Confederation from Carlos.

I admit, by this time, I was really ready for a meal in the sunset, with fellow Unariun students of the Light, which was a beautiful segway to the Cosmic Connection, "A transmission by Archangel Uriel" with her; "Welcome into this great, magnificent Lighted Temple—you have made this possible by your own giving." She was speaking directly to us through Antares, a transmission to help us on our progressive evolution that I treasure in my studies.

I cannot close without expressing my deepest gratitude for Uriel presenting me with a rose, through Antares, that represents her Infinite Love, which leads me to thank Antares for being open to your inspiration, Uriel, for he battled the forces of hell to see this 13th Annual Interplanetary Conclave of Light through to the success you have so proclaimed, which I am ever grateful, the Surprise of My Life.

Arthur Reed

At the Center, Antares' Keynote Address enabled me to tune into my higher nature. Out of these frequencies came inspiration and transcendency to my inner self. It helped me to be open minded and to feel the inflow of Uriel's Consciousness. All the resistance that came to my awareness was now before the screen of my mind, and I accepted it as my own creation. As Marian, Neosha, David Reynolds and Daniel Smith spoke, I felt an inspirational upliftment.

As the day continued, I had a strong feeling: wouldn't it be wonderful if this information about the landing in the year 2001 could be heard all over the world! So it meant a lot to me when, in the transmission from Uriel, it was stated that though only a few people were in attendance at the Conclave of Light to hear the proclamation, nevertheless, it was heard all over the world, psychically!

As this magnificent two-day symposium continued to unfold before me, a realization about the cycle of Isis and Osiris came to my awareness with a sudden psychic shock. In that past, as a companion of Horus, I was in agreement with him and also had a deep hate and resentment for the spiritual teachings of Isis and Osiris. I pretended to be a student of these Shining Ones, but in truth was not. I hated those who were true beacons and bearers of Light.

I took drugs and helped to assassinate Isis and Osiris. It was a horrible and demonic picture that came to me of this time while listening to the lectures. Deep feelings of remorse swelled up within me with a realization that this was the worst cycle in which I had relived fighting the Lighted Beings.

I had a most wonderful uplifting feeling while holding the flag of Planet Din whose leader is Libra. It was a great honor to hold this flag and march in the parade, an event

I shall long remember.

The reading of the Proclamation to Planet Earth inspired my heart with a new sense of gratitude for what Uriel and the Unarius Brotherhood have accomplished—bringing the most positive frequencies to the people of planet Earth.

Just before we were to begin the march, the flag carriers were asked to join in consciousness, to present our polarized unity in the procession of the flags. I had begun to prepare my mind in this way, and relived a past when I felt I had to bless others before public events. I was able to work out this "religious attitude" just before we began to march.

Another tremendous experience happened to me when I viewed the white doves with their little heads sticking up out of the model spacecraft settled firmly on the ground. This tuned me into the time when Uriel took a white dove, kissed it, and let it fly with her Infinite Love. This memory shall live within me always.

The climax of the Conclave was the transmission from Uriel, through the consciousness of Antares. I have been studying the transcript and intend to continue to study it. As a result of this transmission, I had an experience as I walked past the great painting, *The Re-Awakening*. Suddenly, I stopped in my tracks and saw myself with uplifted hands, seeking to be healed of my disease of hatred, resentment, and other negative attitudes that I have created.

I see now why I have been so closed-mouthed and have withheld information about my past. With this realization I felt sick, and only now am I beginning to recover. To think I know it all is a very negative attitude but it is the basic attitude of the priest. I know now that I have been a very ignorant one and did not know anything of spirit.

In sincere appreciation for all the invaluable help that I have received from Antares during this cycle. I know that Antares is my real friend and that the deflations are helpful as I continue my evolution.

Daniel Smith

During the week I was in El Cajon, I felt like I was walking within a bubble of Light. In the Friday class, I could see a white transparent Light-Energy which filled the Unarius Center and I knew Uriel and the Brothers were helping us all to break through our negative barriers created when we brutally murdered these two great Spiritual Forces and thus shut out the Light to planet Earth. The power expressed by Uriel was immense and I was impressed with how the students were able to begin to accept our past and work harmoniously as a group in completing the preparations for the up-coming event.

The positive energies continued to build and both Saturday and Sunday were days to be remembered as each presenter demonstrated their own ability to tune-in to their Inner Self and the Brothers and express a certain facet of the meaning of Unarius and what the landing of Space Brothers from another planet means to the spiritual awakening of the people on our planet.

The whole week spent in El Cajon was very educational and so Light-filled that it would be hard to say what the climax of the experience might have been. When I saw the flag carriers, representing the 33 planets of the Interplanetary Confederation, march around the bend in the road, I felt a shift in my consciousness that was ever so subtle, but I could sense and almost see a golden *aura of energy* fill the atmosphere around all of us. I believe it was a manifestation of the joined consciousness of all our Space Brothers. Then, of course the wonderful dissertation of Uriel at the very end was also especially uplifting to me.

After returning home to Monroe, North Carolina, I could still feel this "higher frequency" for a week or so, before I began to come down to a more normal consciousness. I feel that all of us were stepped up just for attending the Conclave, and I greatly appreciate all the effort and work that went into making it possible.

The world has been infused with a new higher energy and I look forward to seeing what happens next. We all look forward to seeing you soon at the next celebration in February. Love and Light.

Terri Wilburn

I would like to share what a wonderful experience I had during the Conclave.

I felt such a pick-up when I put myself in motion to come to California early to help set things up for the Conclave.

During the time Barbara Jane spoke of the rose, of how Uriel gave it to her during sleep-state, saying "Give everyone my Love with this rose," I felt such a bolt of unusual energy go through me. I felt my skin tingle from my head to my toes, and the love that came forth brought tears to my eyes. I knew I had just had a wonderful jolt of energy from the Brothers, and I was so grateful.

From that time on I could feel a change and an inner peace I had not been able to receive for a long time.

And on Sunday as I was carrying the flag, I felt so proud to be a part of something so wonderful; it was an honor to walk down that road and to represent another world. The energies were just flooding in to me during the entire evening.

I experienced another charge of energy as Antares gave some of the students roses in the tent. Now, as I write this, again the energies pour forth, and I have tears. I thank the Brothers for the opportunity to be a part of something so great and to be joined with students who want to change their lives by going forward.

Neosha

The 13th Annual Interplanetary Conclave of Light had a depth and expansion of meaning to my soulic self as never felt before. The love and light, the tremendous healing power exposed a part of my past that I had cleverly hidden and allowed only minute exposure into my consciousness. This time I no longer could hide as the truth of my past negations swept tornado-like through my being, changing in its pathway darkness into light and allowing me to progress in my next baby step on the progressive pathway.

Within all the marvels of the Love and Light, the healing energies enveloped me into exposing the truth to myself, shocking my systems, bathing all in infinite patterns of rainbow colors and allowing me to see more clearly as the cleansing flames of intense exacting energies removed the obsessions of my own making so that true sight could be restored, enabling me to initiate a change within myself!

My layers of masks were finally removed and I saw the absolute fake I was in portraying myself as a higher being, as a light being, and leading people away from the truth and true Light, away from logic, reason, and the true knowledge of the continuity of life in an interdimensional manner!

What happened in my present life that was a part of those obsessional energies that weakened the foundation of my soulic journey and maintained myself in a static, non-productive, degenerative field? The Isis and Osiris cycle was indeed a very dramatic reliving for me. In this lifetime as I assisted in the care of Ruth Norman, and was at her bedside after she had ascended to her true home on Aries, I had an opportunity to prepare her physical body for its last journey. As I had once so cruelly torn Isis body apart, I now with much tenderness and love bathed for the last time a third-dimensional form, attempting in my own way to wash away the scars and deep wounds of my negative pasts. Her hands had swollen with the degenerative process and her rings now embedded into her flesh, had to be removed. At the time of the murder of Isis I had torn these rings from her fingers, taking with them flesh and blood, but this time I used soapy water to gently remove them. I knew one of the rings was to be given to another student who, during this Conclave, was so reliving her past that she was not present. It struck me at gut level to know I had torn off the ring to give it to this particular student, who now possesses the ring. The ring was thought to have the power to make of its wearer a Light Being! How absurd, as I look at the picture now. But how I must have resented having to give that ring to the present student in that lifetime!

Some attending the Conclave of Light thought that I was Ruth Norman and greeted me with exuberance and overflowing love. I had opportunities to tell them the truth, that I was not she, but if they felt her love flowing through me, then I was most appreciative and grateful for being a channel of her Love. Some of these same individuals, although present those two days, were still heavily involved with wanting crystal balls and attending psychic fairs; the principles in which they were being bathed seem to vanish with where they were going after the Conclave was over. This gave me another opportunity to stand up for Truth and gain more insight on how I led people astray with my life as a fake and fraud. I was really hit at gut level and just wanted to hide someplace!

I had an opportunity to join a caravan to the landing site for the first practice of the Flag March. The landing site, although portrayed as a picture of positive changes, looked like a field of destruction to me. The poisonous oleander beckoned with their pink blossoms as I gingerly wended my way down the hill, limping and balancing as a wounded soldier. I sat down ready to review the troops. As the march began, I was thrown into a time warp and those participating appeared as tired illusions from the past. The final Parade of the Flags was beautiful, inspiring, and I had to choke back the tears that flowed freely. I had so much wanted to be one of those who carried a flag, but had to face the reality that no longer was I physically able to march. That day I felt the Muons from Myton enveloping me as I sat down. They too, had a different mission towards the Interplanetary Confederation and their light and love followed through my eyes of spirit.

Having been chosen to speak gave me the opportunity to relive being a fraud and fake in the past, allowing myself to be presented as a light force, when indeed I was not. The Battle of Armageddon ensued in the weeks prior and a fear struck the core of my being! Fear exploded within, as now I was to be truly exposed before the universe!

Overcoming the negativity gave me many moments of closeness and unity with the Muons on Myton, and many times tears just flowed with their light and love projected into my being. The blinding, bonding force, between Planet Myton and Planet Earth, is Uriel. Her magnanimous Love entered my consciousness, overwhelming me into a transcendency in a way I had not felt before. When I had finished my short speech, I was told by many present that my face lit up with light and love as the power embraced me and, for those moments, I knew this to be true. Inside I felt like such a fake, such a failure. I had failed my progressive evolution! I had failed Uriel! I had failed Antares! As people came forth to tell me again and again how strongly they felt the power, I only felt the failure within myself, the ego deflation of being exposed as a fake from my past! I relived to the fullest my failure and experienced the feelings of accumulated guilt for choosing the wrong direction and leading so many souls astray. One person asked me with the greatest sincerity, "Why did you leave Myton?" I told her that I had chosen a regressive path. For a few moments I had felt that awesome oneness with the Muons, and then my mind became a blank!

Yes, the Conclave of Light was, to my being, a Conclave of Light, Love, and healing energies. This power uncovered, within the depth of my being, energy wave forms that have prevented me from taking my next steps into a light-filled future. Saying I am grateful for every moment only touches the surface of my appreciation. I knew Uriel was present along with the members of the other 32 Planets of the Confederation, the Muons, and Brother Alta.

The tent gave me an opportunity to experience troops dying of cold and hunger, and the wounded lying about. I was then lifted into a transcendency that surpassed all third-dimensional understanding as Uriel, through Antares, brought us a message of hope, of her Love and Light, ever beckoning us along the pathways that penetrate interdimensionally energies from life to life in the process of becoming a light among Lights, to be of service to mankind!

Don Wilburn

I just received your phone call to congratulate Dan on his write-up. Your encouragement to me to write up my experience during the Interplanetary Conclave had a spiritual force behind it, and I am prompted to act on your advice.

My negative reliving started some weeks before the Conclave of Light. My mental outlook had a sleepy drowsiness which served as a blocking off to my inner senses. My interest level, spiritually speaking, was at an all-time low, or all-time high on the physical side. My conversations were repeatedly becoming subjective, which was a regeneration of a very negative past during the Isis and Osiris period.

The closing week of the Celebration approached with a video from Lani which was very descriptive of how the flag carriers were to march to their designated area. This represented the plot to destroy these two Master Beings, as far as I was concerned. I was a participant in the slaying of Isis and Osiris, and the evidence was being presented more clearly once I arrived in El Cajon.

I went to the landing site early Sunday morning to help Frank Garlock prepare for our celebration and was immediately shocked when I saw what appeared to be the bodies covered over with an artificial grass covering blanket. This gave me the final proof of my involvement.

Prior to this event I had been questioning some of the teachings, and because I was oscillating in a negative field of energy, I was beginning to believe I did not have freedom, which prompted me to seek out excuses for quitting this Science of Life. This was the re-expression of negative energy from that particular past that settled over my consciousness like a tight woven net, which was producing that all time spiritual low. I know that having participated in this very negative act that my guilt would overwhelm me, so I sought out a way of justifying my deeds, and this took on the form of finding fault with their teachings. My method of doing this took on the design of proving that their proclamations were false, which was also a part of my consciousness in this present time. I was a very devious person in the past and wanted company to go along with my misery, so I resorted to my own declarations, stating that Isis and Osiris were frauds with harsh judgments that imprisoned man's mind, eliminating people from the opportunity to live normal lives, and we should liberate ourselves permanently from all their teachings.

In teaching and proclaiming this as truth, a great distortion developed in my consciousness which was the gateway to dissolving my spiritual alertness to Spirit and has been my downfall so many times in the past.

As I was flying back to North Carolina, I still had not recognized why I was maintaining such a low state of consciousness; it was sticking to me like a two part epoxy glue. The feeling I had was not something enjoyable; it had a very distinctive contrast to what I had been developing into for the past 10 years or so. The depth of my reliving was so deep that I was able to see only one course of action. I remembered the joy and contentment that always accompanied me when studying the basic course of Unarius. This I have been doing since I returned to North Carolina, and I'm now once again free of the insensitive type of mentality.

So thank you Antares for encouraging me to write up this overcoming, it finalizes the loops.

P.S. *Infinite Perspectus* was the book that helped to lift me up above the reliving, because it reveals the falsity of false teachings.

The Re-Awakening

The skies cleaved open,
    the night was rent,
And heaven-streaming, blinding Light
    flowed cascading down
Upon the sorrow-stricken soul,
    bands of healing Love
Encircling him in gold;
    the softiest, whitest doves of peace
Flock'ing forth in joy!

The Re-Awakening

Now the tale can well be told
    how the battle long was waged
Light touching Dark,
    Dark fighting Light
Through the eons
    ever on, the battle raged.

'Til the victor–Uriel–
    was seen to raise a Lighted hand.
"Awake!" she cried,
    and the Demon gave way,
Fell there on bended knee
    and wept!

The skies cleaved open,
    the night was rent,
And heaven-streaming, blinding Light
    flowed cascading down
Upon the sorrow-stricken soul,
    bands of healing Love
Encircling him in gold;
    the softest, whitest doves of peace
Flocking forth in joy!

The war had ceased! The battle done!
    "Awaken ye all! Rejoice!
For Uriel has healed the Foe,
    the evil in each demon soul!"

She fought with Love
and only Love,
Led the Angel Forces
to the very pits of hellish fire

On, she fought, against hate and fear
and mortal wounds,
No thought for self, no time to cease
and bide another day

Her eyes agleam with Life
she saw but one possibility -
That of victory!
the rescue of one soul lost
And dying in its smokey grave,
one soul that drew behind
The chained remains
of many more

Ever on, she sought him out,
returned again, again, again
'Til the dawn began to break
and demon thoughts turned to
Half-breathed whispers in his mind

"Uriel," he heard, and turned away,
'Uriel' - the name again passed through
And ever did it echo there
'til he could bear no more!

"Uriel!" he cried in anguished pain -
the name meant more in memory!
"I know that Light, that radiance!
I know this soft touch
Upon my brow!"

"Uriel," he begged upon his knee,
    "I know you are the One,
The Angel Force that can rescue me
    from self-built hell,
Dear Angel, Uriel!"
    And as he turned his tear-streaked face
To seek above a sign,
    there in flowing gown of halo light
Did Uriel appear!

A cosmic symphony of softly flowing Love,
    a galaxy of stars,
A Being pure beyond the scope
    of mortal sense,
For she is nothing less
    than Life itself -
Formed and shaped as human-like
    so we can see her eyes!

For from them flows the sea
    that washes guilt and shame
And hateful ire
    in the harmony of Truth
Its salt does sting
    the self-inflicted wounds,
Yet Peace comes behind
    to gather up and nurture back to life
The starlight Self within.

"Arise," she said in loving joy,
    "Come walk with me anew!"
And as the chimes rang clear the songs
    of all Infinity,
The Demon's heart did burst
    and fall away!

And in its place, a new-born life,
    an opportunity unmatched,
To free the bonds of many more,
    To sing the song of victory -
For this one conquered naught but self,
    with Uriel to hold his battle sword
When wearied arms began to slow.

His joy met hers,
    a victory so vast
That only as the lion
    shares its berth with tender lamb
Will man conceive
    and raise aloft his own heart
And seeking mind -

"Uriel!" he'll hear in harmony,
"Uriel can set you free!"

Billie Mc Intyre

My first awareness of being in the Isis and Osiris cycle, was when Carol asked David Hogue and myself to go to the landing site and pull weeds from around the area where the "Welcome Space Brothers" sign is located, for it was to be the site where a film crew from Los Angeles would film the future area of the landing of the Brothers in 2001. This was in the late spring or summer.

As I pulled weeds, I threw them over the side of the bank. Soon I realized that I was drained of energy; I would pant for breath and have to stop and rest. Also, the sun was hot, and it would make me dizzy. I finally stopped to ask myself, "What am I reliving?" I looked up to the spaceship sign on the hillside and knew it represented the spaceship that had come to pick up Isis and Osiris to take them back to their home planet. Then I knew what the weeds represented to me. They were the people I was murdering and tossing aside in that long ago frenzy of killing in the hot land of Egypt.

As time went on through the summer, I had many aches and pains all over my body. My legs felt as though they had been yanked from my body, my hands had many cuts on them from cutting flower stems at work, and my head would hurt off and on. I knew this was what I created for myself when I wielded a knife against Isis and Osiris, murdering them, and pulling their limbs from their body, with the aid of others. I was jealous of them and crazy for my own power; I wished to take their place. I wanted what they had, and I stole some of their possessions in the aftermath of the murder.

Another time, when this cycle was in-phase, we were filming a psychodrama about this period in Egypt. I was relatively new to working out my past karma. On this occasion, I was handed a knife to hide in the folds of my robe, and when Uriel came down the hillside to the middle of the crowd, I was terrified at what I saw. The guilt was so strong within me that I could not move, and the tears did flow. Uriel was always so wonderful to show us what we needed to work out our past. But I was too guilt-ridden at that time to do anything, except to know that I was guilty and wait for another time or times when this cycle would come around again. And it did.

Another cycle was on the Interplanetary Confederation Day when we all paraded down the street to the city park, by the library. I was a Guardian Angel, all dressed up with a sword and shield and marching right behind the Space-Cad, which carried Uriel. After this day was over, I knew that I was part of the personal guard that was to protect them. This was a turning point in accepting my guilt a little deeper. After that we never had to wear the Guardian Angel costumes again.

Now back to the present cycle. The negative forces were very strong within me. I felt the obsessions, like bats descending from hell descending upon me. It was hard to move forward because there were many blocks set up to deter me. My body was tired, and it was hard to motivate it to do anything. Right up to the last minute, before the Interplanetary Conclave of Light celebration, the blocks were strong.

David asked me to pick up his flower order on my way home from work, but all they gave me were the roses. I wrote out the check and then realized that there had to be more. So I asked the man if there was more to the order. He said no; so I bought some greens to go with the roses and left. When I saw David at the Center Friday night, he said there was a whole bucket set aside with Unarius written on it, and would I please return and get them, because he had no time. I got in my car, but two blocks away my car stalled. It took at least five minutes to get it started, but it ran so roughly that I returned to the Center. My first thought was that I didn't really need to get more, that what we had would be enough. Margaret offered me her car; I hesitated a bit, then said yes, and took off to pick up the flowers. David asked if I would stay to help him. I said, I needed to see whether my car would start before I let Margaret get away. It started, and I stayed.

I stopped to think about each thing that happened, and knew that if I let the negative win out, I would be helping to deter the positive efforts and regenerate my past. So I stayed calm through it all and came out feeling really good. I knew that each of us had to overcome our obstacles so the weekend would go well.

This was the first year I can honestly state that I was really looking forward to this weekend. I awoke on Saturday morning, feeling eager to go to the Center. It was a most powerful day, even though another block was thrown at me when my car was towed away in the middle of the morning. I ran out to see if it was gone and, for the first time in my life, I was not angry. My thought was that this was another attempt to bring down my conscious-ness by the negative forces, and I must stay calm and all will be fine. This was really a first for me. I returned to the Center and forgot about it until the lunch break. When I went to pick up the car, and I had a reaction to the impound fees, but got over it faster than usual. Antares stated that the cars being towed away represented the owners having been abducted.

The afternoon was even more power-packed than the morning. I loved every minute of it. When I awoke Sunday morning, I had a new feeling about me. I had an inner feeling that we had crossed the line of our past and were entering the positive future that Uriel had always promised us. I was even more eager to start this day. I went to the Center and was surrounded by video cameras.

I was talking to another student when I noticed a camera was panning my body from the bottom up. I was taken by surprise, just for a moment. Right after that, another couple asked me if I would explain the model of the Future City to them for their camera. I walked to the model city and the lady asked my name. Then she said, "Oh, you are the one that painted *The Re-Awakening*." I began to tell her of my experience with Uriel and Leonardo. When the busses were readied, we hurried outside. They said, "This was even better than hearing about the city."

On the bus trip to the land, I started to wonder what I was reliving with all these camera people, and with the excitement that I felt. I then realized what it all meant. I was also reliving my abduction; the trip on the bus was to another planet and all the attention by the press was the effort of the abductors to find out all they could about the society that I came from. I was still excited and looking forward to this new adventure. I also realized, in a more in-depth way, what it was like to experience the loss of all one's possessions and to be removed from familiar surroundings.

It had taken every cent I had to get my car out of the impound, for it cost me $111.00, which was outrageous. With this experience, I saw my part in reverse. Now I was the one being abducted. I had to put the shoe on the other foot. I relived the rest of it when, after dinner, we all sat in the tent (an internment camp for refugees). When Antares didn't enter to give the dissertation on time, I started to get an uneasy feeling—all was not what it seemed to be. Of course, this was just the reliving of finding out that I was not a guest of another planet, but a prisoner.

As I alighted from the bus, I had the same excitement that I had had all weekend. As I stood waiting for the parade down the hill to begin, the music began to play, it brought tears to my eyes as I thought about the Brothers and realized that, on the Inner Worlds, they had already landed their craft. It had already happened; they were here already in spirit. This was so uplifting that I could hardly see because of the tears. The parade down the road was wonderful. I felt the Brothers on all the worlds present. I still had the feeling of being in the future. When the doves were released, I teared again, as I do every year. Uriel stated that we were on the positive side; this was nice to know, but for once I already knew it.

On Monday, I arose and felt like it had been already a week since the Conclave celebration. I needed to go to work, but I was feeling "unphysical." Reality came back when I awoke on Tuesday or Wednesday with a headache. I was really sick, but I still had to go to work because I was painting a large mural for a show and no one else could do it for me; I had another one to go and a deadline to make. I went through three days feeling sick without even asking, "What am I reliving with the fires that are burning out of control throughout the county. After a moment's thought, I realized that I had been reliving burning people in the cities of Egypt, which I had done in more than one cycle of time. I was still reliving the aftermath of the Isis and Osiris cycle—the rampage of death and destruction. Then I felt better.

In spite of all the negative reliving, I can feel the positive power of the future. I know that I will have to work harder to maintain a forward trajectory into the future. I can really appreciate what Uriel and the Brothers have gone through to bring us to this time in our evolution. Thank you, Brothers, for not giving up on us, and thank you, Antares, for being a true channel for Uriel. I can feel the difference with the love you project.

Tracey Kennedy

This Interplanetary Conclave was the best ever. Each year I learn more about myself, and each year the celebrations get better and better. Without a doubt, the highlight of the weekend was the Flag Procession. It was spectacular beyond words. The setting at the land was and is perfect. It was beautiful watching the Space-Cad head down the hill followed by the trumpeteers and the flag carriers, in which I took part. Prior to beginning the procession, Lani suggested we take a mental journey and tune-in to the planet we were representing. I psychically saw the people on planet Po gathered together for a celebration and projecting to us on Earth. I felt so honored and privileged to carry a flag for this planet. Tears ran down my face the whole time in appreciation for what was happening.

In reflecting upon this experience and previous years, I can honestly say this is the first time I had no concern for self during the procession. Many years ago, I was so nervous that I would be "found out" by someone I knew, filmed, and seen by someone, embarrassed and humiliated, that I secretly dreaded carrying a banner. Each year I have worked to understand the negativity and opposition to the Brother's landing. Although I know I still have much work to do, I can see some progress, which helps propel me forward so I, too, can be a positive force for the Brothers of Light to land on planet Earth.

I was so excited when I sat in the tent during the transmission with the realization that this is the first class in the University of Unarius on Planet Earth! It made me appreciate Uriel's inspiration to buy the land and Antares' receptivity to having the celebration there.

In the weeks that have past since the celebration, I have

come to realize that this event is still transpiring. Every time I think back on the positiveness of the weekend I am transcended again. I feel a newness about myself and a "lift" in my consciousness. This is only the beginning, and I can't wait for the future! Thank you Brothers!

Dorothy Ellerman

It was evident this beautiful sunny day in October at the landing field that the Unarius students were being well-prepared for this life-changing event—the arrival of Space Brothers on Earth in 2001. But even more than that, we were day-by-day shedding our lifetimes in reverse of Truth!

So each and every Conclave of Light, initiated by Uriel and the Brothers of Light, gave we students the opportunity of not only shedding our negative past lifetimes through the teachings of the Unarius Science, but as important, giving us knowledge of the future ahead, in preparation for the landing of starships of Light in 2001 as well as those ready earth inhabitants.

Positive energies fill my soul as I think of each and every Conclave of Light which Uriel, the Cosmic Visionary, has proclaimed for the benefit of this earth world, so in need of peace!

Yes, students around the world are being prepared as each day brings us the opportunity to use the Unarius principles involved in this life-changing study.

Beatrice Morse

When I recently was a participant in the 13th Annual Conclave of Light held in Jamul, California, something occurred within me which I will continue to reflect upon and carry with me for quite sometime.

Being a nature-lover, I could appreciate fully the vastness and serene grandeur and stillness that surrounded me as I stepped from the bus. As we began to gather for an attunement before the celebration, I began to feel the nervous excitement that I had felt in recent years when I carried a flag. Absent, however, was the severe debilitating pain that was identified as sciatica and arthritis some time before, and was then located in my hands, hip, legs, and back.

During those years Mrs. Norman, Archangel Uriel, was with us in the physical, and she briefly mentioned, in a note sent to me, that these were negative oscillations in my psychic anatomy, often occurring in the autumn years. Not really comprehending what that was, I continued to study past-life therapy as a practical tool in my personal self-healing, attending classes in El Cajon whenever I was able to do so. Now, waiting for the celebration to start, I was participating in a much healthier way, without the symptoms as they had presented themselves in previous times. I was feeling magnanimous and a part of something greater than myself, a Universal Family of Man. In my own way, I sent a welcome to the Brothers and Sisters who would be coming from distant planets to usher in the true Age of Enlightenment and Spiritual Renaissance, the so-called Age of Logic and Reason in 2001. The Higher Beings have progressed themselves and are practicing concepts as taught by the Unarius Brotherhood.

The trumpets sounded as the Space-Cad proceeded down the hill. The "aura" seemed very brightened. The vibrant colors of the flags, the music as it resounded, together formed the perfect setting for the Arrival. After each flag carrier was presented to the audience and had formed a semicircle around the mock starship, another student stepped up to the ship. Gently he lifted the top and 33 white-winged doves were released. As they circled overhead, forming smaller vortexes, then larger ones, they surrounded all of those present before they finally flew off carrying their regenerative messages and serving as 33 polarities of universal peace and brotherly love.

During the transmission, as I sat under the tent I felt at peace within myself and with the group that assembled there, not feeling claustrophobic as I sometimes do when among larger groups of people. It was hard to believe that only a few weeks prior I had such feelings of apprehension and fear when I went up to the land with others to rehearse for the event. I had a realization later, in a class session, that my fear was remorse started from negative energies when I opposed my higher self and committed crimes against myself and my fellow man. Yes, it is a crime of destruction when we put out negative thoughts because, as the universal law of cause and effect, it will rebound upon us; and although I did not understand all of what I was suffering, my willingness to remain open to Spirit, as I have sensed it to be, was now thought forms that still remain. This I would begin to attempt self healing with the Unarius Science of Life.

As the bus drove from the street through the heavy fog that had developed, I felt comfort and warmth, as if I was wrapped in a healing blanket of energy, less fearful, and a knowing that I was not alone in the universe.

Since the celebration, I experienced a releasement, as I related unresolved traumas resulting from a situation which I incurred when I had chosen not to abort a baby that I had conceived, and chose to adopt. I was a single, unmarried woman at that time. This releasement was catalyzed at the time Antares had related to me that my biggest overcoming would be when I could open up in front of the group in class. I certainly had not planned on it being as soon as it turned out. That night in Wednesday class, as I sobbed and sobbed, I felt the Center fill with warmth and I was able to receive so much love in a silent way, feeling no judgment from the other students. That is the great experience, being able to heal oneself by taking personal responsibility and participating in your own healing, thus helping release others whom I have harmed. I was able to trust myself and in my way tune-in to the Higher Beings who I have always known, on a very deep level, were the guides that have always protected me when I so willfully went against them and denied their existence, thus putting myself through so much turmoil and causing family and friends to suffer because I thought I was God. I just had to do things "my way" which, of course, was not the best way. Now, sharing my own personal experiences and applying them along with the science of energy as taught by the higher Beings on lighted worlds, I am able to truly help myself and begin to release myself from the destructive energy which, through my self concern and self-centered behavior, really boomeranged upon me as mental illness in this life. I am proving, in my moment-to-moment interactions with the people I meet in my daily life that, in order to have true psychic liberation, one must be totally honest with oneself, accept personal responsibility, and not put the blame for one's problems on someone else.

Socrates said, "Know thyself." Self-understanding is what I have always longed for in this life. I am very appreciative, as I have stated in class more than once. I am proud to be a Unariun, realizing that I don't have to make any big, big splashes to be recognized, and that if I am sincere in trying to understand myself and willing to change, that I am contributing to the Infinite. I am doing my best in a more positive way.

Monica Appel

As a member of the Unarius choral group, And the Angels Sing, I sang the song "A Whole New World" at the Interplanetary Conclave of Light. After my participation in the Conclave, this song took on a new meaning because this memorable event truly opened "a whole new world" for me. My experience of the Conclave was analogous to experiencing the future, and "what a positive future it will be!" as Uriel has told us so many times. The feeling of transcendence and inner peace, the clearness of mind, the feeling of interconnectedness to all people, including the peoples on the planets of the Interplanetary Confederation, and the feelings of Love I experienced were wonderful! I felt truly "alive" and more aware than ever of my purpose while living on this earth planet.

The opportunity to participate in the Interplanetary Parade as a trumpeteer has always been a thrill. This year I listened to the proclamation and realized the reality of the Interplanetary Confederation like I never have before—the reality of my personal responsibility in the preparation for planet Earth to become the 33rd member of the Confederation. Also I realize the importance of maintaining a positive state of consciousness to welcome our Brothers and Sisters from the other 32 worlds.

With the acceptance of my involvement in the brutal killing of the Light Beings, Osiris and Isis, and my opposition to Spirit, I appreciate more than ever the opportunity that I have been given to turn this past around by becoming an active participant in such a positive event. I recognize the opportunity I have been given to become freer and more open to Spirit through my application of the principles of past-life therapy. I understand the need to know myself.

My experience of the Conclave means a new beginning, a new commitment to my spiritual evolution and to the mission of Unarius. During the two days of the celebration, I was open to the Light and Love of the Brothers like I never have been before, an experience that I will never forget! It will serve as a barometer to measure my present state of consciousness, to strive to reach this higher mental state more often. I look forward to being a part of a positive future, to a whole new world filled with Light and Love.

Ronald Breault

In giving of self at the land, all along the last two months of preparing for the Conclave, I was aware of my resistance to the Mission. I did not care to pass out the large flyers, but I did it anyway, and I learned from this experience where I've been in the past.

When the hard work of clearing the land was completed, I was very appreciative of all the students who had helped to make sure that the Conclave would be successful. The hard work and sweat was more easily accepted because I knew, by my positive work, that my psychic load was becoming lighter. I became aware that I was releasing my guilt from destroying the mission and the Brothers of Light. Now, I was turning that around.

I was not concerned for myself, but was only concerned that the Mission move forward. I felt the Love from the Infinite, therefore it was a worthwhile cause. I felt great joy that my past was getting lighter as I recognized my part in this negative cycle of Isis and Osiris. I appreciated the privilege being given to me, and to be able to turn this past around.

During the two-day celebration of the Conclave, I was feeling very transcended. When I was marching, during the procession of the flags, and had turned the bend on the road, I looked toward the starship and my eyes began to water. I felt the Love and the healing energies of all the Brothers on all the thirty-three planets that we were representing. I was thankful and grateful to be given this chance.

The Monday and Tuesday following this weekend, I was still transcended. But I miss this group consciousness and wish this love feeling could last forever. It will, in the future, and I am looking forward to this time.

Thank you, Uriel, for all the Love and help.

David Hogue

Like most experiences of a transcending nature, I have not yet been able to truly appreciate them for the positive influence they have had on my life. Well, it was no different this weekend at our 13th Annual Celebration of the Interplanetary Confederation.

On Saturday, up at the landing site, I got really angry at William. But later that morning, in riding back to the Center with him—I had ridden up with him to the landing site—I noticed that the anger was no longer there! The anger was gone because I was no longer in-tune with the same feelings. I was indeed surprised because this doesn't always happen that quickly for me, if ever!

After the transmission on Sunday, I had the strongest urge—and William will tell you that I would normally not have done this—to walk over to him and give him a big friendly hug! So I did! A further proof of how strong the power was this weekend.

I had another uplifting experience on Sunday afternoon. During the Parade of the Interplanetary Confederation, I carried the flag for Polarity Link of Planet Farris. Before the parade, I was mentally asking Link questions of a personal nature because of something I was going through at the time. I suppose you could say that this helped me to create a "link-up" within my consciousness for the following experience. While the proclamation was being read, I felt as if I was being lifted right out of my body! In listening to the words, I could actually feel or sense, for that brief moment in time, the reality of the Space Brothers landing upon our planet in the year 2001!

Thelma Fletcher

As I gather my thoughts and place them on the 13th Annual Conclave of Light, I become transcended as the events of the two days pass before me. How can I put into words what this celebration means to me? This was the culmination of five months during which time I experienced many realizations, relivings, workouts, and healings. I began to see the past in a much closer way and the cold-blooded, cruel, crazed person I was in that lifetime. I stooped to every vice possible to accomplish what I wanted—stealing, plotting, lying, bribing, drugging, and eventually murdering. There were many incidents and relivings that put me deep in the middle of this cycle: relivings with patients, co-workers, family, and fellow students as we worked on our projects.

On Saturday morning, bright and early, we greeted our many friends from all over the country—not a stranger among them.

Antares opened the day with loving words and inspiration. We were then treated to a wonderful series of presentations by students of Unarius. What a power-packed day it was. We were thoroughly imbued with the energies of the Light.

Sunday was a special day. When we arrived at the landing site, we soon after began our flag procession. I could feel the tremendous power, even the walk up the hill with the flags seemed more like floating. It was with a great deal of love and pride that I carried the flag for Susa, the leader of Planet Endinite. I could feel his presence and the love he carried to this celebration.

The dinner was lovely, and it was wonderful to dine in the fresh clear air of the mountains. The evening's agenda was filled with love and light.

Uriel's transmission was incredible. She was so close to us all. The reality of a starship landing seemed more possible to me than ever before. My resistance is weakening, as I can finally accept my part in the horrendous crimes against Isis and Osiris and their followers.

This was a weekend I shall never forget. I felt I was truly, in the eye of the Infinite, a small but happy grain of sand. I was happy to be here, happy to be a part of this wonderful mission to return planet Earth to its rightful place in the universe, and happy to be able to help those I have harmed and regain my place in Infinity.

Decie Hook

I have had a fear of writing my report because it might be rejected as not being honest enough, not being open enough. But there is a part of me that says I must "stretch the envelope," and not let fear, failure or tardiness stop me, but to push forward with all my might, for I will feel guilty if I don't at least try to make an effort.

I stayed up until 2:30 a.m. last night typing this. Then I turned around and deleted the file. I couldn't sleep; I was so angry at myself. This morning I had a big cry. I dragged my feet doing it in the first place, which I realize now was my resistance to spirit—just like at the time of Isis and Osiris. Then deleting the file showed my staunch resistance—it showed me how deep this resistance really is. I am going to overcome the lower self by finishing this report.

The Interplanetary Conclave of Light weekend was phenomenal for me because of my brutal, horrific past that came out and the opposite polarity, an incredible feeling and sensing, a peek at the future.

First of all, what stands out for me is being a sales person, being accessible for people to purchase Unarius books, audio tapes, video tapes, posters, cards, starship emblem pins, etc., at a display table another student had set up. I was proudly admiring it when Antares came along and said, "Decie, that table should only have one of each item displayed and the rest in the office for you to get when needed." At first I grumbled mentally, "who does he think he is?" Then I caught myself and my negative attitude which was my attitude toward Seth at the time of Isis and Osiris. I decided to be positive toward and with him and take his suggestion happily and graciously. After all, he isn't Seth anymore. I then said, "Sure Antares, I'd be happy to." I did the task joyfully leaving just one of each item. I stood back and looked—wow! It looked so beautiful; it radiated light—not because I had done it, but because I was open to Antares, who is open to Spirit, and it was transferred through frequency-relationship from Antares, to me, to the display table. It was proof to me that if you're open, a so-called task can be easy, and the results positive.

The first speaker was Marian Keymas; she spoke from the heart and with great enthusiasm. I, for the first time, could feel and know that Commander Star and President Godman really do exist; just as do the Muons from planet Myton. I cried and cried with this realization and the overwhelming Love I felt from them. In reading the book *Preparation for the Landing*, it only seemed like science fiction to me but, as Marian spoke, I could feel their collective love projections to all, preparing each and every one for the great advent which will take place in 2001.

As each speaker gave their presentation, the energies grew and grew and so did my transcendency. I thought the roof would blow off the Center with all that power and the uplifting enthusiasm of the speakers themselves. It was truly a great light-filled day and evening. I didn't think it could get any better, not until the next day.

Sunday was incredible. It started by getting the flag carriers ready, with their sashes and planet buttons in place, before they got onto the bus. I realized my anxiety in getting everybody ready, and just right, and on the right bus, revealed my participation in the murder of Isis and Osiris. In the past I made sure everybody was "in" on the murder, the plan outlined just right, and everything covered. I wanted absolutely nothing to go wrong; we must take over and have total control—thus my anxiety and obsession with everything being perfect and timely.

On the bus ride up to the land, a camera crew was interviewing a new person. I was reacting at first. My thoughts were, "He's giving misinformation; he doesn't know anything about Unarius or about spirit." I said to Lani, loud enough for the crew to hear, "Tell them you want to be interviewed." Then I caught myself and I realized the new person mirrored to me my ignorance and misinformation, both in this Egyptian past and in the present. I felt ashamed of myself. I thought, "okay, let's make a positive out of this experience." So I looked over at Lani and I did a thumbs-up sign—let's tune up and be a positive polarity for him. We both did a change-about in our consciousness. He said some things that were really touching and inspiring, and were proof that he had been touched by spirit; that's why he was here and taking part.

Then we pulled onto the property in Jamul. We entered the gate and I had a breakdown, crying, seeing through past eyes the murder scene all set up at the time of Isis and Osiris—beautifully. I thought, "who would ever know such a heinous crime would take place here? It's so lovely, and peaceful and peace-filled."

Then we disembarked and all picked up their respective flags. All of we flag carriers joined together as Lani took us on a mental journey to the higher worlds. I couldn't appreciate it at first because I got tuned into a general, "hyping" the troops up for battle. This was a trick I had used previously of sorcery and hypnosis to control my men in combat. Then, after that realization, I could enjoy the journey.

We all joined in consciousness! I could feel all the Brothers with us, the Muons, the Confederation denizens, the higher Brotherhood—we were all one big family of mankind—joined as one! It was so overwhelmingly profound and joyous! As the music resounded, the trumpets pronounced. With the Space-Cad so eloquently in the lead, we started processing. The tears flowed and flowed as we all walked together in unison, proudly displaying our Brothers' planets and their leaders' names; proclaiming there is life out there, and we are all joined as one!

I felt as if I were floating; I was so uplifted! I couldn't even feel my feet touching the pavement. Then Kevin pronounced each planet one by one. Truly, I don't remember what was going on because I was so uplifted and transcended. I remember the doves flying out of the starship and circling to the beautiful music. Round and round they flew—one moment their white wings shimmered in the sun's rays and then they seemingly disappeared. Then their white wings shimmered again in the sun's rays and again, they would seemingly disappear. It was as if they were oscillating in and out of the third dimension. It was like watching 33 starships glistening and shimmering. Truly it was one of the most spiritual highs I have ever experienced! I felt I was flying with them!

Then, at the end of dinner, Antares came and sat at our table. I thought I'd faint, the fact that he would sit at the same table with me and visa versa. I was stunned and shocked, and speechless. I know now that I was fearful he knew my thoughts, just as I was fearful that Seth knew my thoughts, because my thoughts toward Seth were ones of murderous intent. Seth spoke his mind, just as Antares does, but for different reasons. Antares speaks truth, sometimes painful to a big ego like mine, but he says it with love. I have proof he speaks with love in his heart because I have felt it, and it has helped me to see some things about myself I didn't want to see. But I reaped the positive benefits; therefore, I am grateful.

But according to my account of Seth, he said things to intimidate, control, to put people down (at least in my eyes this is how I felt). I couldn't wait to get rid of him because I knew I wouldn't be accepted in the new order, in the new government of Egypt. I wanted someone in power who would help me to get power, to accept me. So I sat there, fearful he would know how I felt, and would know I helped to murder him in that life. I was trying so desperately to hide what I was broadcasting with every fiber of my being.

Then, we had the transmission, which was beautiful and inspiring. When the roses were given to students who had worked hard, both physically and psychically, I felt small and deflated, and let down. But, I knew truly within I didn't deserve one. I've been a laggard, physically and psychically. "It's time to change!" Those were the words I heard while sitting there. And I certainly had enough encouragement, light and love all weekend to help me out of my lethargy.

Thank you Brothers for this wonderful peek at my future. And thank you, Antares, a Brother of the Light who has helped me greatly, although I have fought and kicked, and screamed all the way while learning of a better way. Thank goodness, Love conquers all!

Marian Keymas

I want to express my deepest appreciation and gratitude to you, Antares, and to Uriel and the Unarius Brotherhood, for the most beautiful Interplanetary Conclave of Light ever! The weekend of October 12th and 13th was truly a most Light-filled, radiant, magnanimous event, touching every soul present with the highest Love frequencies.

I want to express my most sincere thank you to you for extending to me the most wonderful opportunity to speak on Saturday and to co-facilitate the workshop on Sunday with Dan and David. I just cannot put into words how I felt. It brings tears to my eyes just to think about the privilege that I was given. Thank you for the honor and the privilege to be a channel for the Brothers. No other thing on Earth could mean more to me, or be more important.

I had a wonderful experience as I sat in the audience. I felt the most incredible power flowing through me, from the top of my head to my toes. This love and power brought me to tears. I sat there and cried as this beautiful love flowed through me. I knew that Uriel was right there with me, cradling me in her infinite Love. Words cannot describe that experience.

The flag parade at the landing site on Sunday was the most magnificent ever! As I marched as a trumpeteer beside the Space-Cad, the tears flowed from my eyes as I felt such love and high frequency energies. I realized the great significance of the flag parade of the 33 planets, which really impressed upon me the reality of this Interplanetary Confederation. The pristine landscape was the perfect setting, as the atmosphere was free of all the mundane noise and clatter of the city.

I want to convey to you, Antares, my appreciation for the transmission you brought through. There is so much to be gained and learned from studying it. I have read it several times and will continue to study it. It says it all. As you said, we are the most fortunate people on Earth to have been given this once-in-a-lifetime opportunity. I just cannot say enough about it.

I look forward to seeing you tonight for Sunday class. I love you!

Carlos Redhead

In this overview of my attendance and participation in the Interplanetary Conclave, 1996, I will share some of the most enriching and meaningful experiences that I had. My particular purpose in making the trip to El Cajon at the invitation of the Unarius Director was to actively participate in the event as a presenter. I saw it as an opportunity to give of myself to the Unarius mission, that wellspring of life from which the knowledge of the Infinite is drawn. Through the last 20 years of my Unarius upbringing these studies have given me jet take off in my spiritual ascendancy. But it has also provided a learning curve whereby the tools of knowledge and usage applied as a continuous refining process are learned of and utilized.

Left to my own resources, I would say that, because of the scheduled dates for the event and my extremely busy schedule in my workday world, it seemed that it was not the best time for me to travel. I was physically tired due to other time schedules and the long workdays which stretched into nights. In fact I would be due to fly out from Toronto after returning on the last flight from Ottawa just a few hours before with no more than two hours sleep. However, my focus was on getting to California, so the airline bookings were made. I would leave on Friday and return to Toronto on Monday. While this seemed practical for me, I also knew that the combination of time difference, jet lag, and distance, meant I would be demanding more from my physical energies then I might have.

Then an incredulous event occurred. My airline tickets were being dropped off for me but in confirming the travel dates by phone, the agent indicated I would be leaving one day earlier, on the Thursday. This was perplexing. This would be the Canadian Thanksgiving Weekend and air travel would be busier than normal. Furthermore, should I not leave on Friday as originally planned, I would have to use up an extra vacation day and put my workload even further back upon my return.

Unariuns, however, have become accustomed to the way in which Spirit moves. This ticketing error turned out to be no accident. The agent went off to try to rectify the problem, and I thought "What if?" What if no Friday flight could be found? In that instant I had a deep insight that the whole purpose of the trip would best be served if I left matters the way they were. The next reflection I had, was that I would need the extra day in El Cajon to settle down and get extra sleep, otherwise I would not be able to function adequately with a body that would keep calling attention to itself. And as often happens, when guidance is needed with a positive, spiritual, purpose at stake, both the help and the solution become manifest. Immediately I lifted the phone to call the agent and gave instructions to leave the tickets as they are. The next thing that happened was, the Brothers shined a pearly bead of light through my consciousness as confirmation of my response to their gentle, inspirational prodding. Here was a demonstration of purpose, motivation and intent, all being streamlined synergistically into one focus, to help make the Conclave a success.

There was yet another difficulty that I had to face and work at overcoming. I was experiencing the discomfort of my left hip joint. It seemed that the closer I got to San Diego Airport the more persistent this discomfort became. It was not a new pain, but it certainly changed from being an on-again, off-again situation, to one of more constant concern.

By Sunday, the big day, I would need to be in attunement for the major talk in one of the final sessions of the Conclave, but I was now almost limping. No one observed it. Two evenings before the Conclave, when I attended a Friday class at the Center with more than 30 students, we knew very precisely that we were in the Isis and Osiris cycle. On this score I had given a realization which I will relate shortly. However, the question I had to focus on with my hip became, "Was this part of the same cycle whereby my hip is carrying, so to speak, a karmic memory of one of several dastardly acts committed against the Lighted leaders of Egypt?"

My time for addressing the gathering was getting closer. By now I was bent on staying calm and seated, hoping at best to rest the hip. An Unariun learns to go within to seek all answers and to never ask to be relieved of some condition without examining the terms of its reliving relationship with the past; that condition of self, that establishes our own responsibility.

However, at the Friday class to which I referred, Monica, another student, mentioned the word skin in her relating. That one word generated much significance for me, because that very morning while I was putting on my socks in the motel room, I was attracted to some skin marks above my right ankle. Although I knew the origin of these marks, (the remnants of old mosquito bites incurred in the early summer) this particular morning they seemed to startle me. In my mind they took on the thought-reality that they were nails or spike holes in my lower leg. The flash came as a clear mental image of a heavy club studded at the larger end with sharp spikes.

Here was evidence for me of the Isis/Osiris cycle that reminded me of my karmic load. What one does to another is done to self. That is principle. This was my grim reminder of the corrupt part I played on that hilltop in Egypt, when as part of a mob gone wild with the selfish, egotistical desires for power, I had attacked the Noble Ones with this club. The bodies were not only deflated of the breath of life but the senseless, frenzied attack continued till limbs were dismembered and flesh and skin torn. (As I write this now, I still feel more releasement). The tie into this lifetime also rang on another note for me, because I also recalled that earlier that day while in the company of Antares I fought to resist the urge on at least two occasions to say to him, "Why don't you put some olive oil on that patch of dry skin on your forehead?"

Those events had led up to the Sunday in question wherein I was in pain in the region of the left hip. I placed my consciousness to dwell on how I felt and why. I seemed to focus on the notion that this pain that I felt represented the pulling apart and dismemberment of the limbs of the Noble Ones. Sometimes we block ourselves off from facing the truth because to our ego it is too horrible to accept and my concern at this time was to attempt to get at the true answer to the question, "Did I pull or rip or cut away the leg?' Sometimes these answers do not come about immediately. The sense that I got was that although I feel I did not participate in this particular activity, I still incurred a guilt from seeing it done by the group to which I belonged.

That Sunday evening I had no cause for concern. The pain ceased. Several minutes before I was introduced to the podium the pain had vanished. I could serve in my capacity free and clear of any physical concern. I can say that as I write this account over a month later the pain in the hip has not recurred.

The positive experiences that I had during the Interplanetary Conclave were numerous, but I will briefly share one other with the reader which was most meaningful for me and also provided a demonstration of the efficacy and mastery of these Teachings brought to our planet by Uriel, Raphiel and the Unariun Brotherhood and which library is still being built. These talks, delivered without a script under the auspices of the Brothers who inspire and prompt the nature of the concepts to be articulated to the audience, are usually delivered from a higher mental plane. Somewhere in the middle of this talk a fly decided to drop in on me. This was a persistent fly. It was intent on coming up to my face, it even touched me once, but the greatest curiosity I had about it, was that it buzzed like a bee in my ear. The lower astrals can be very devious in their ways in trying to short circuit a positive effort. I brushed it away but it kept coming back. This was obviously causing me to lose my hookup because my conscious mind was now becoming engaged. I lost my attunement.

I stopped. I had to, because no more thoughts flowed. I had nothing to say. My connection with the Brothers was cut off due to the distraction and the lowering of my consciousness. This caused me some consternation. "Should I walk off the podium?" The blood was rushing from my head as I began to feel faint. "No," I thought, "Purpose must be realized, and if I relax without anxiety and could open up my consciousness again, the Brothers would never let us down."

And so I calmed myself, stood there and waited. It may have taken some minutes, but soon the alignment was made again and the power was even stronger. I can also add that the faces of the students and guests in the audience throughout this time, reflected a positiveness and harmonious rapport. Their energies also helped to cement the re-engagement and dissipate that interfering thought form made manifest. Indeed we were altogether, on one frequency, caring and sharing.

For the growth opportunity in the contact with Spirit I show my gratitude as a student, to Uriel who overshadowed the weekend's events; to the Brothers for always being there when there is the need, and to Antares for being an excellent Teacher and Guide, one who sometimes teaches eloquently without words spoken. A most successful Conclave!

Samantha Walsh

Just a Thought Away

An even day's time
breathing out
breathing in
Involuntary motion
opens the eyes
and closes them, then

Thoughts—like a train
on a never-ending track
involuntary?
Who decides?
Going where?
Going forward? Going back?

Just a thought away
lie dimensions
of grandeur and grace.
Just a thought away
lie dimensions
of grandeur and hate.

Once upon a mind's reflection
I saw a world, a people
of wondrous perception

And then, another's thought
   protrudes, interrupts,
   people of darkness—caught!

Just a thought away
   Where is my mind today?
   This moment—where?
Just a thought away
   are masses of intellect
   full of love, armed with truth.

Just a thought away
   are hordes of like minds
   vultures true, vampires too.
Such a fine line . . .
   Where are you?
   Which "thought" do you choose?

         With the help of
         Alfred, Lord Tennyson

A Transmission From Archangel Uriel

"Dear students of the Light, you are welcomed into this great, magnificent Lighted Temple; you have made this possible by your own giving, by your work, and by your new attitude. You reap what you sow.

"Today is the first day of the next many days that you will have, not only on this earth but on future earth worlds. In your future will you live in the light of your new psychic body, a body that you are beginning to update, to polarize, so that you will have the capability to live on the spiritual worlds where light is the nature of life. There is no darkness; there is no envy; there is no violence; there is only an understanding of each and the others' purpose in evolution to advance the knowledge of the reality of Spirit.

"Spirit is Infinite Intelligence. Infinite Intelligence is Light, which will make manifest each person's progressive evolution, whereby he will be a giver of self; she will be a giver of self, and the she and the he will be joined as it must be to polarize both facets of the Self, the interdimensional Self that is the polarized reflection of the Cosmic Mind.

"Yes, this is true! We know that you cannot yet conceive of these abstract principles of energy. However, if you continue on with your progressive evolution, you will begin to understand and apply the interdimensional principles of consciousness in your future lifetimes. That is to say, your psychic body or electronic body will evolve to be in-tune with the higher frequency necessary in attaining cosmic consciousness.

"The Infinite Creative Intelligence is not a He; It is not a She, It is not an It. It has been alluded to by earth people as God, the Father, the Christ Self, Brahma, Allah, etc. But these words are still only names that cannot substantiate the omnipotent and omnipresent nature of the Infinite Creative Intelligence. When you have conceived of the reality of the higher self, you will then experience your at-one-ment with your inner self, just as you know when you are out-of-tune with your inner Self but are too concerned with and emmersed within the lower self to admit the truth of the gravity of your situation.

"But let it be said that today marks the first day in the positive up-going of events for planet Earth. On this day, the 13th of October, the celebration of the annual Inter-planetary Conclave of Light has healed those undesirable elements that had become a patch-quilt of negative deeds, which have been a major factor in the past which has caused serious problems with humankind. The nature of this problem has been a breakdown of the spiritual, gossamer body, the mind, which had lost its direction by becoming mired in the deserts of earth civilizations. In this way did the individual and society become separated as islands in a vast sea; each island completely and totally separated from the other, and all of them separated from the Mainland, which designates the spiritual nature of life.

"Yes, this is true, the reason why there is such unrest on your planet is because there is no direction. The Light has not been shining, and your ships have been crashing against the shoals of your land, and you have gone adrift. But now the reawakening has come upon humankind. Such a reawakening is of the paranormal nature of consciousness, the intuitive faculties of the mind. Therefore, when one becomes aware of the higher precepts of consciousness, it is likened to awakening from a deep sleep.

"Such a deep sleep was caused by psychic amnesia, a forgetfulness that was a construct of the subconscious due to memories which remind one of the past and which were so awful that the blinds were pulled down.

"Psychic amnesia was caused by having opposed indi-viduals who were teaching about progressive evolution; the continuity of life after death; the continuity of consciousness, life after life; and the reality of Spirit as the creative effigy of Infinity. Such opposition was, in fact, an opposition to the spiritual Generator, the faculty of the higher consciousness developed by those individuals who are known as Brothers of Light due to their progressive evolutionary development. Brothers of the Light have mastered their lower selves and, as such, are Avatars who are known as Archangels, Cosmic Generators, who project the Light of logic and reason throughout the universe. You know them now as Raphiel and Muriel, Michiel and Uriel. Gabriel and other light bearers work in other areas of the universe.

"It is the universal understanding of science that is now the basic need for the direction that life must take on the plane on which you presently live ensconced within a five-sense atomic body, for a reason of course. The physical body is a property of the Infinite, but it is not the only property. It is not the only factor of Infinite Intelligence; it is only one-half of the wave form, one-half of the polarity.

"The Infinite has its true identity as an alternate current, which Nikola Tesla brought to recognition in his application of these interdimensional principles of energy within the construct of electronics. The great electronic development that he initiated in the early 19th century and the 20th century has brought light to humankind, albeit it is a light that shines as a demodulation of the electromagnetic flux field that is the basis of all sun systems in the galaxies and universes in the third dimension.

"But, using the vernacular of your civilization and culture, after all things are said and done, and we have talked about the abstract concepts, we must get down to business. That business, which is the bottom line, is the recognition of self. Who am I? What am I? Where am I? What is my purpose in life?

"Who am I? That really is the most important question that could be asked of anyone, and especially should it be asked of oneself because, truly, one does not know oneself until one has pushed into the very interior of that which we call "self," into the psychic anatomy, a word not as yet recognizable in the vocabulary of your twentieth-century civilization, but one which was known in the prehistory of Earth.

"Psychic means non-atomic, therefore it must be other than a physical factor or a physical thing that you can touch, taste, feel, hear, and smell. It is the interior of oneself that our Brother, Jesus of Nazareth, called the "kingdom within"—and for good reason. It is a kingdom not made of the material elements of your world. It is not made of the ego elements of your world; it is not made of the boundaries that limit such a kingdom unto itself. It is an infinite kingdom, and it is the property of each individual.

"Yes, you have a vast kingdom that you own, because it was and is and always will be the creative effigy of the great infinite Cosmic Mind that bestowed this kingdom upon each one! And yet you do not know of its existence. Isn't that a shame that you do not know that you contain the Godhead, that you can effect anything that you wish because you have the potential to construct a positive future for yourself!

"Not constructing a positive future, you automatically construct a negative future because you contain, in this kingdom, the alternate features of it. This is the polarity factor in which life functions—forward and backward, up and down, in and out. There is always this alternate picture, which is the necessary means of making sense out of nonsense; it is called analysis! You probe; you ask; you look backward and forward; you look in and out, so to speak. You apply, and you learn to apply, and you learn to understand this application of logic because logic is the construct of Infinite Intelligence.

"A reasoning person is an intelligent person! A person who asks questions is an intelligent person! A person who is caught in the claptrap of belief systems that were constructed from ignorance of the principles of interdimensional physics is not intelligent. Therefore, if one accepts these constructs of old belief systems, old wives tales and superstitions, one is caught in the trap of a lower dimension and cannot begin to use the precepts of his mind. One who has not learned of his own nature thinks that someone else has the truth. He becomes simply one of the followers and is taken along the garden path listening to music that enthralls him, but which takes him away from his true self.

"So the bottom line is knowledge of self! It is the bottom line in all that we are effecting and doing in the preparation for the landing of our Brothers, our Space Brothers from the Pleiades, one of the physical planets in the Milky Way Galaxy in the constellation of Taurus. This contact will bring home the reality that not only are there hundreds of trillions of billions of humankind doing their thing, living their lives and learning of themselves—particularly of the inner self and of their spiritual contact with Cosmic Intelligence—but you are seeing, in every respect, the reflection of yourself when you have the capability to reach beyond your small or large ego self and realize that there is more to life than you have ever imagined.

"Our Brother Shakespeare put it very well when he said, 'looking into the mirror, darkly'—which translated means seeing the negative factors of oneself in that mirror, another aspect of the polarity principle. That which we see outside of ourselves is the reflection of what is inside ourselves! We are always looking at the mirror and seeing a reflection of ourselves. One man or one woman sees the mirror reflection and says, 'How beautiful! I have never seen such beauty! It's transcending; it really moves me beyond my own problems!' Another says, 'What an awful scene. What awful people these people are. How could they do this?' He or she has seen but a reflection of himself or herself. Beauty knows its own radiance. You cannot see beauty in another person, place, or thing unless you see it in yourself, unless you have activated it!

"Today, the 13th of October 1996 on your plane, will mark a great demarcation in the preparations for receiving other human beings who have made a greater contact with their inner selves. You have already seen Space Brothers on Earth; you have seen, felt, and touched the visage of Uriel, who lived through the body of Ruth Norman; of Raphiel who lived through the body of Ernest Norman; of Michiel who lived in the body of Nikola Tesla. You have seen pictures of Leonardo da Vinci; you have seen pictures of Michelangelo; you have seen pictures of Albert Einstein and of other philosophers, teachers and avatars, poets, scientists, and many, many more of whom we can not speak at this time. You have touched the hem of advanced humankind, but you have treated them as if they were similar to yourself. You have only seen a reflection, a reflection of yourself. Very few people have recognized the Godhead in another individual because they have not recognized it in themselves!

"And yet, when Commander Star and his people exit from their spaceship, not only will you see and feel the rising of a 'sun,' but the entire planet will be raised in consciousness because the Sun has actually set upon Earth. That Sun lives in these one thousand people who have activated the properties of Infinite Intelligence. They have individualized it—and that is the purpose of evolution! When you say that you want to be well, that you want to be healed, you are touching and tasting and feeling what it means to be separate from your infinite Father. Healing is the recognition that you have separated yourself from your own Infinite Self. You see, the Father lives within you; the Father is not an outside configuration!

"We are not in this celebration for the sole purpose of

verifying the reality of extraterrestrial life forms, spaceships, and what we would call space vehicles. We are celebrating the fact that the curtain, which has closed planet Earth from other habitable planets, is rising! This has been a development of some hundreds of thousands of years. The Hierarchy of the Unarius Brotherhood manifested physical anatomies on planet Earth in order to project the Light to humankind in important cycles when the Light was being dimmed due to the negative force that was being expressed. Uriel is the manifestation of Infinite Intelligence and carries within her polarized consciousness the intelligence of the spiritual Hierarchy. The Infinite Intelligence that is the Cosmic Consciousness of Uriel overshadowed the physical incarnation of Ruth Norman to wake up those who were seeking for the Light from their dreamstate, so that they would see the beauty and reality of life.

"You see, as you begin to awaken, you will have these experiences when you leave your body during sleepstate. When you leave your body for your astral life to begin a cycle there, you will learn what it means to be a radiant being; you will meet your teachers and see them in the reality of their own consciousness. You will see the real clothing that they wear; it is the clothing of their psychic anatomy, an electronic configuration more radiant than all the fireworks on the Fourth of July, so to speak. This energy is infinite; it can be viewed anywhere, anytime, anyplace, in any part of the universe; but you need 'new eyes' to see; you need 'new ears' to hear and that is the purpose of this the Age of Logic and Reason.

"You will learn how to 'see.' You will learn that the conscious mind is only the small self, and this self needs to view life in this third dimension, on terrestrial planets. This is an evolutionary mandate in order to gain experience, in order to analyze, in order to separate the wheat from the chaff, in order to eventually polarize that experience so that the energy is so polarized that it will be a part of your higher consciousness, which is an electronic circuitry.

"Such polarized facsimiles of information are positive because the information is aligned with Infinite Intelligence. It contains the immortality of its intelligence; therefore, it cannot be destroyed and will regenerate infinitely!

"There is no death, as death is only a limited knowledge of one's understanding of the interdimensional nature of consciousness. Life that is lived will be lived with great understanding, based upon the experiences one has gained and the ability to know what direction to take when the red light goes on, when the green light goes on, or when the orange light goes on.

"You see, we cannot tell you and give you the secrets of immortality; we cannot tell you what the Infinite Creative Intelligence is—if it is anything; we cannot tell you about the great constructs that manifested as cities and towns. We cannot even explain or even out-picture in your mind how a flower is grown, how it is created. The reason is, my friends, that it is all in the mind! So you must know what this mind stuff is in order to appreciate the realities that are still in your future.

"Presently, everything that you see that you cannot understand, that is a puzzlement to you is called an anomaly; it does not fit into the four squares. You have not learned, yet, about the vortexal nature of all things, and that the vortexal nature is a constant movement between the macrocosm and the microcosm, and that it is an interchange of energy. The macrocosm, let us say, is the positive polarity; the microcosm is the negative polarity.

"Eartheans are living in the microcosmic part of Infinite Intelligence. The macrocosm is an extension of the microcosm. The microcosm is the negative polarity, and the macrocosm is the positive polarity of Infinity. Viewing the microcosm with a microscope and the macrocosm with the telescope dazzles the mind, to see the magnificent star systems that are truly galaxies, and to understand the nature of these lights. The vortexal relationship between the two polarities is difficult to conceive. Your conscious mind cannot perceive this abstract concept because of the rigidity of old belief systems, which are mental constructs. Those mental constructs are of such power that they create walls more rigid than steel; they create your belief system which is the steel that binds you within the limitations of this present inability to see.

"But, we are not here to lecture you, but to congratulate you. You have learned something today and you have learned that anything that has a positive aspect to it is made up of the substance of finite particles. A molecule is made up of atomic particles, and of course the atom is made up of elemental particles, quarks up to the electron, and then the so-called atom which is a configuration of energy. And yet, the atom can, by its collectiveness and its association, be created into molecular forms, associations of atomic forms of whatever they may be—hydrogen or oxygen atoms—and they become molecules of this substance. Each are purposeful to develop a cellular structure, which again in the conjoining of cellular structures, develop some particular component of a physical anatomy, or a tree, a rock, or a flower. But it takes the collective whole of these parts, particles, to make of that which is a component of its part—a heart, a lung, and eventually the physical anatomy of an incoming spiritual entity, a human being. For this human being to function in another part of the Infinite through a physical anatomy, it takes the great intelligence of the Creative Infinite and, of course, the intelligence of advanced, intelligent Beings who are a part of this constructiveness. The physical body itself is an example of the great intelligence that has been imparted from the Creative Infinite!

"This means that you contain all of these factors within yourself, but you have looked in the wrong direction for answers to your life. The answers can only be found by looking within. Your language, even, is changed. You do not blame your present situation on outward configurations. You do not look for your transcendencies and your good health from somewhere else. You heal yourself! In this respect you must learn of the reality of the infinite equation that lives within yourself. And yet, it is not that simple either; there is a great deal of work involved.

"Since we are all part of a great whole, a grand whole that has been given the name, the Grand Design of Life, we will find that each planet is a part of this design. As we look into the heavens and see the sparkling lights and realize that there are, according to your astronomical equations, two hundred billion sun bodies in your Milky Way Galaxy, then we can appreciate that since there are hundreds of millions, if not billions of galaxies, there must be untold trillions of sun bodies with untold quadrillions of earth bodies and planets that orbit these sun bodies!

"The Infinite Creative Intelligence did not create one small planet and put dumb animals upon its floor. The Infinite Creative Intelligence is out-picturing itself in its finite manner and way! This is what the Age of Logic and Reason is about. A change is coming about on planet Earth; it is a change within each individual's understanding of the interdimensional design of life!

"Now Uriel has given the greatest of her Energies as she lived through a physical body. A physical anatomy is a receiver. The transmitter can transmit continuously, but the receiver does have to shut down from time to time to shore up its batteries. So the receiver does find in some respects a certain incapacity as it has continued to receive information and sends its information out to the far corners of the earth world. This is what Ruth Norman and Ernest Norman have done; they have given of themselves and they have died for the earth people, life after life, in their objective to help humankind learn to recognize their spiritual design.

"The celestial consciousness of Raphiel overshadowed Ernest L. Norman and Jesus of Nazareth when they lived on Earth. Ernest L. Norman therefore, to all intents and purposes, relived and was the reappearance of Jesus of Nazareth. The proof of it is in his works, the books that he has written to explain the teachings of Jesus which were, and are the teachings of Unarius in the scientific idiom. Ruth Norman, Mary of Bethany, the betrothed of Jesus relived her life with Ernest L. Norman and continued in this polarity relationship as she did 2,000 years ago, to advance the knowledge of the reality of reincarnation and to introduce the concepts and principles of reliving or the principles of healing oneself, known as Past-life Therapy.

"Ruth Norman gave of herself and died for the earthman hundreds of times! She extended her tenure on Earth to the age of ninety-three so that those who were being helped to continue the Mission would be able to see, with eyes open, the reality of their past, to polarize their past lives lived as renegades against the Light; so that they would be good role models and champions of the science of life teaching, lived by all people on non-atomic worlds of a higher frequency that are fourth-dimensional in design. To live on a higher-frequency world of Light, where there is no darkness, one must know of one's spiritual nature. Ignorance of the interdimensional function of the mind would result in being obsessed by lower astral entities, just as an airplane would be pulled down by the force of a hurricane.

"So we are celebrating the positiveness, the spiritual substance of those who were involved in the planning and in the completion of the 13th Annual Interplanetary Day Celebration. The positiveness happened because each person was working together, each with the other. You are proving the principle of polarity relationship. Therefore, you have gained a great learning, and you have advanced a step in your positive evolution. This will never be forgotten because it is constructed of positive energy. It is information that will become a strong part of your next step, to develop your paranormal ability to see with new eyes.

"Yes, there has been a joining, a joining between the lower elements of life and the higher elements of life! Spirit truly entered into the earth world during this celebration when the 33 facsimiles of the Interplanetary Confederation were seen out-pictured in the physical sense, marching to the landing site with the triumphal chorus of the trumpeters. The proclamation to the earth world is such that, although it was read in a more or less inaccessible area of planet Earth, it was heard psychically throughout the world!

"Believe you this! I speak to you as Uriel, my friends, my children, students of the Light. I was known as Ruth Norman when I lived on Earth. I am in all ways, in every way that can be imagined, overjoyed by the success of this 13th annual celebration of the landing of spaceships on Earth. We have worked hard to bring you up to this point so that you could enter into this great positive expression.

"When the curtain opens, humankind will become more than a 'kind.' Rather, each individual will recognize the reality of their spiritual energy and of the joining of themselves with other humans who live on extraterrestrial planets.

"We Brothers of the Light have always known that this cosmic event would take place in 2001! We have been planning for it for many hundreds of thousands of years. Now that planning has been brought to a fruition! This is the first step! Yet that first step needs to be heralded and shouted, if you wish, to all four corners of the earth and to the heavens above!

"You have now developed a foundation. Do not be surprised with the many new contacts that will be made! Everyone will want to get upon the bandwagon, but they cannot. They must change their frequency first. They must become humble in the knowledge that they are a pearl, a link in the great chain of Beings.

"The Interplanetary Confederation represents the Mind Energies of the 33 Logoi, advanced, intelligent Beings in-tune with Infinite Intelligence. This explains the substantial ingredients that are the substance of the pulse of life, which is the interactive relationship between atomic and non-atomic planes of life, continuing into the higher celestial and supercelestial planes, and even beyond.

"Infinite Creative Intelligence cannot be conceived. The Cosmic Mind can only be outpictured to the extent that one is capable of conceiving the abstract principles of interdimensional physics. Yet each person, each soul, contains the substance of their Infinite, Creative Intelligence to develop the ability to tune in to the higher precepts of their consciousness, enabling them to feel the overshadowing influence of the higher Beings who have attained cosmic consciousness in the inner worlds.

"You people, as you well know, have been caught in the ice age of Tyron, the central planet of the Orion Empire 800,000 years ago, and you have not been thawed out completely. There is still some work to be done, but at least that obsessional past is being out-pictured, and thus objectified, and thereby you are healing yourselves of the disease of ego.

"Remember this day, dear friends and students of Spirit! Remember that this day is the first day of the next days of your life! Live in the Light and you cannot go wrong. Listen to your Heart. Be a friend; reach out and you will always be encircled in my Love, which is everlasting!

"To say the least, I am proud of those students who gave of themselves. They have earned a 'step-up' in consciousness. It is only in this way, through the hard work of working out past-life negative experiences, that you can make the next step-up in your progressive evolution. I thank you. Love! Love! Love!"

Unarius Academy of Science
Jamul, California
October 13, 1996

Addendum

Now that you have had an opportunity to read about the activities of the Unarius Academy of Science teaching about the nature of consciousness, an interdimensional science of life, you may wish to receive additional information about this life-saving, healing science of the Spirit and the Mind.

Please address your inquiries to the Unarius Academy of Science, 145 S. Magnolia Avenue, El Cajon, California 92020-4522. You will receive the 48-page, illustrated introductory booklet, Pathway To Light, a National Public Access TV Guide listing the Unarius programs shown on twenty-five stations throughout the United States, and a copy of the Unarius Light Journal, published quarterly.

Unarius carries on its activities throughout the world with active Centers in the following cities:

Unarius-International Center   Tel: 1-800-475-7062
Charles L. Spiegel, Director   Fax: 619-444-9637
145 S. Magnolia Avenue   Internet: www.unarius.org
El Cajon, CA 92020   E-mail: uriel@unarius.org

Unarius-North Carolina   Tel: 704-283-5077
Daniel Smith, Director
2603 Rolling Hills Drive.
Monroe, NC 28111

Unarius-Florida   Tel: 407-734-1939
Joyce Inge, Director
8853-A Andy Court
Boynton Beach, FL 33434

Unarius-Canada   Tel: 905-874-9262
Carlos Redhead, Director
4 Hart Street,
Richmond Hill, ON L4C 7T7
Canada

Unarius-Canada   Tel: 905-874-9262
Clifford Holland, Director
330 Nill Road So. Suite 410
Brampton, ON L6Y 3V3
Canada

Unarius-Africa   Tel: 234-82-232-134
Nwabueze Adirije, Director
Box 910 Orlu Road
Owerri, IMO State
Nigeria, WA

Unarius-New Zealand   Fax: 64-4-382-9802
David Cole, Director
Trojan House
125 Manners Street
Wellington, New Zealand

Unarius-Spain   Tel: 91-352-15-56
Robert Goodman, Director
Quadalquicir, 20
Pozuelo-estacion
28224 Madrid
Spain

Unarius-Italy
Athos Ubaldi, Director
Via Aselli 33
Milano, 20133
Italy

BOOKS AND VIDEOTAPES
By The Unarius Academy of Science

BEGINNERS GUIDE TO PROGRESSIVE EVOLUTION, Ruth E. Norman & Charles Spaegel, 369 pgs., Hardcover

BRIDGE TO HEAVEN, Ruth E. Norman, 434 pgs., Hardcover

BIOGRAPHY OF AN ARCHANGEL, Ruth E. Norman, 373 pgs., Hardcover, Also on audio tape

COMMUNICATIONS FROM OUTER SPACE, Ruth E. Norman & Charles Spaegel, 470 pgs., Hardcover. Also on audio tape

CONCLAVE OF LIGHT BEINGS, Ruth E. Norman & Charles Spaegel, 583 pgs., Paperback, Also on audio tape

CONFESSIONS OF I, BONAPARTE, Louis Spiegel, 540 pgs., Hardcover

COSMIC CONTINUUM, Ernest L. Norman, 163 pgs., Hardcover, Also on audio tape

COUNTDOWN TO SPACEFLEET LANDING: Tesla Speaks Series, Vol. 7, R. Norman, 186 pgs. Paperback, Also on audio tape

THE EPIC: Tesla Speaks Series, Vol. 13, Ruth E. Norman, 290 pgs., Hardcover

EXPLORING THE UNIVERSE WITH STARSHIP VOYAGER. Ruth E. Norman, 533 pgs., Hardcover, Also on audio tape

GRAND DESIGN OF LIFE FOR MAN, Vol. 1, Ruth E. Norman, 500 pgs., Hardcover, Also on audio tape

INFINITE CONTACT, Ernest L. Norman, 188 pgs., Paperback Also on audio tape

INFINITE PERSPECTUS, Ernest L. Norman, 188 pgs., Hardcover Also on audio tape

BOOKS AND VIDEOTAPES
By The Unarius Academy of Science

INTERDIMENSIONAL PHYSICS, Ruth E. Norman, 320 pgs., Hardcover, Also on audio tape

THE LAST INCA: ATAHUALPA, Ruth E. Norman & Charles Spaegel, 345 pgs., Hardcover

PATHWAY TO LIGHT, Charles L. Spiegel, 44 pgs., Paperback

THE PSYCHOLOGY OF CONSCIOUSNESS—A WORKBOOK, Charles L. Spaegel, 22 Spiral-bound lessons, Also on audio tape

PREPARATION FOR THE LANDING, Ruth E. Norman & Charles Spaegel, 500 pgs., Hardcover, Also on audio tape

MAN, THE REGENERATIVE EVOLUTIONARY SPIRIT, Ruth Norman & Charles Spaegel, 345 pgs., Hardcover, Also on audio tape

MY 2000-YEAR PSYCHIC MEMORY OF MARY OF BETHANY. Ruth Norman, 74 pgs., Paperback

PRINCIPLES & PRACTICE OF PAST-LIFE THERAPY, Ruth E. Norman & C. Spaegel, 434 pgs., Hardcover, Also on audio tape

THE RAINBOW BRIDGE TO THE INNER WORLDS, Ruth E. Norman & C. Spaegel, 391 pgs., Hardcover, Also on audio tape

RA-MU OF LEMURIA SPEAKS, Ruth Norman & Charles Spaegel, 511 pgs., Hardcover

RETURN TO ATLANTIS, Ruth E. Norman & Charles Spaegel, 325 pgs., Hardcover, Also on audio tape

RETURN TO JERUSALEM, Ruth E. Norman & Charles Spaegel, 286 pgs. Paperback

THE SPIRITUAL DANCE OF LIFE, M. Teri Daunter, Ph.D. 220 pgs. Hardcover

BOOKS AND VIDEOTAPES
By The Unarius Academy of Science

TESLA SPEAKS: Vol. 1 Scientists, Ruth E. Norman, 347 pgs., Hardcover, Also on audio tape

TEMPUS PROCEDIUM, Ernest L. Norman, 480 pgs., Hardcover, Also on audio tape

TOUCHED BY LIGHT, Ruth E. Norman, 130 pgs., Paperback

THE VOICE OF VENUS, Ernest L. Norman, 197 pgs., Hardcover, Paperback, Also on audio tape

YAMAMOTO RETURNS, Dennis Dallison, Paperback & Videotape

YOUR ENCOUNTER WITH LIFE, DEATH, & IMMORTALITY, Ruth E. Norman, 75 pgs., Paperback

A LESSON COURSE ON SELF-MASTERY, Ernest L. Norman, 13 videotape series An advanced course describing the basic principles of evolution.

THE ARRIVAL—Video, An encounter with the Space Brothers, a story of reincarnation, Lemuria and Orion 59:00 min.

THE INTERPLANETARY CONCLAVE OF LIGHT, Videotape series 1996 2-day Symposium, Lectures and Ceremonies

LEMURIA RISING—Video, A psychodrama of the civilization of Lemuria re-enacted by students of Unarius 53:00 min.

SOULIC JOURNEY—Video, The past lives of Ruth Norman 55:20 min.

THE UFO EXPERIENCE—Video, A panel discussion with seven persons who have had vivid personal contact with UFOs. 52:12 min.

TRUE TALES OF ISIS AND OSIRIS—Video, A psychodrama. Isis speaks about Love to her students. 46:20 min.